On the Job English

English for
MEDICAL
PROFESSIONALS

Practical English
Communication Skills for
General Medical Professionals

CARROT HOUSE

On the Job English -
English for Medical Professionals

© Carrot House

All rights reserved. No part of this publication may be reproduced, stored in a retrieval system, or transmitted in any form or by any means without the prior permission in writing of Carrot House.

Printed: August 2020
Author: Carrot Language Lab

ISBN: 978-89-6732-322-6

Printed in Korea

Carrot Global Inc.
9F, 488, Gangnam St., Gangnam-gu, Seoul, 06120, South Korea

Curriculum Map

Course	Level 1	Level 2	Level 3	Level 4	Level 5	Level 6	Level 7	Text Book
General Conversation	Essential English : Begin Again; Pre Get Up to Speed 1–2	New Get Up to Speed+ 1–2	New Get Up to Speed+ 3–4	New Get Up to Speed+ 3–4	New Get Up to Speed+ 5–6	New Get Up to Speed+ 7–8	New Get Up to Speed+ 7–8	
		Daily Focused English 1	Daily Focused English 2					
Discussion				Active Discussion 1	Active Discussion 2	Active Discussion 2		
					Dynamic Discussion	Dynamic Discussion	Dynamic Discussion	
			Chicken Soup Course	Chicken Soup Course	Chicken Soup Course			
				Dynamic Information & Digital Technology	Dynamic Information & Digital Technology	Dynamic Information & Digital Technology	Dynamic Information & Digital Technology	
Business Conversation	Pre Business Basics 1	Pre Business Basics 2	Pre Business Basics 2					
			Business Basics 1	Business Basics 1				
				Business Basics 2	Business Basics 2			
					Business Practice 1	Business Practice 1		
						Business Practice 2	Business Practice 2	
Global Biz Workshop				Effective Business Writing Skills (Workbook)	Effective Business Writing Skills (Workbook)			
				Effective Presentation Skills (Workbook)	Effective Presentation Skills (Workbook)			
					Effective Negotiation Skills (Workbook)	Effective Negotiation Skills (Workbook)		
					Cross-Cultural Training 1~2 (Workbook)	Cross-Cultural Training 1~2 (Workbook)		
					Leadership Training Course (Workbook)	Leadership Training Course (Workbook)		
Business Skills				Simple & Clear Technical Writing Skills	Simple & Clear Technical Writing Skills			
				Effective Business Writing Skills	Effective Business Writing Skills			
				Effective Meeting Skills	Effective Meeting Skills			
				Business Communication (Negotiation)	Business Communication (Negotiation)			
				Effective Presentation Skills	Effective Presentation Skills			
					Marketing 1	Marketing 1		
						Marketing 2	Marketing 2	
						Management		
On the Job English				Armed forces 1	Armed forces 1			
				Armed forces 2	Armed forces 2			
				Aviation 1	Aviation 1			
				Aviation 2	Aviation 2			
				English for Cabin Crew				
				English for Call Centers				
				English for Medical Professionals				
				English for Aviation Maintenance Technicians	English for Aviation Maintenance Technicians			

※ This Curriculum Map illustrates the entire line-up of textbooks at CARROT HOUSE.

CARROT HOUSE

English for MEDICAL PROFESSIONALS

Introduction

Carrot House Methodology

Andragogical Approach & Productive English

The teaching of children (pedagogy) and adult learning (andragogy) are distinctly different. Pedagogy is akin to training and encourages convergent thinking and rote learning. It is compulsory, centered on the teacher and the imparting of information with minimal control by the learner. Andragogy, by contrast, is about education as freedom. It encourages divergent thinking and active learning. It is voluntary, learner oriented, and opens up vistas for continued learning. Adults need to feel independent and in control of their learning. Therefore, Carrot House curriculum is based on andragogy and is designed to encourage learners' participation and engagement by providing more task-based activities and opportunities to frequently interact in the classroom.

People want to achieve communicative competence when they learn other languages. English education in foreign language environments has been rather focused on the receptive skills of English—listening and reading—which simply increases learners' knowledge about a language, not the competence of using it. If people are well equipped with productive skills—speaking and writing—they will be competent in English communication. This is why Carrot House curriculum is designed to enhance learners' productive skills throughout the course. This andragogical approach of the Carrot House Curriculum, which focuses on productive English, will enable learners to achieve communication skills necessary for global competence. Carrot House's teaching philosophy and curriculum combine to provide a "Language for Success" for all learners.

Communicative Language Learning (CLL)

This communicative interaction, the essential component of language acquisition, does not occur in a typical, non-meaningful, fun-oriented conversation with native speakers. It occurs in a negotiated interaction through which a well-trained teacher provides the comprehensible input that is appropriate to the learners. The learners, at the same time, actively utilize the opportunities given to them by the teachers.

To this end, the Communicative Language Learning (CLL) method is employed in the field of Foreign Language Acquisition. The CLL method provides activities that are geared toward using language pragmatically, authentically, and functionally with the intention of achieving meaningful purposes.

Unit Composition

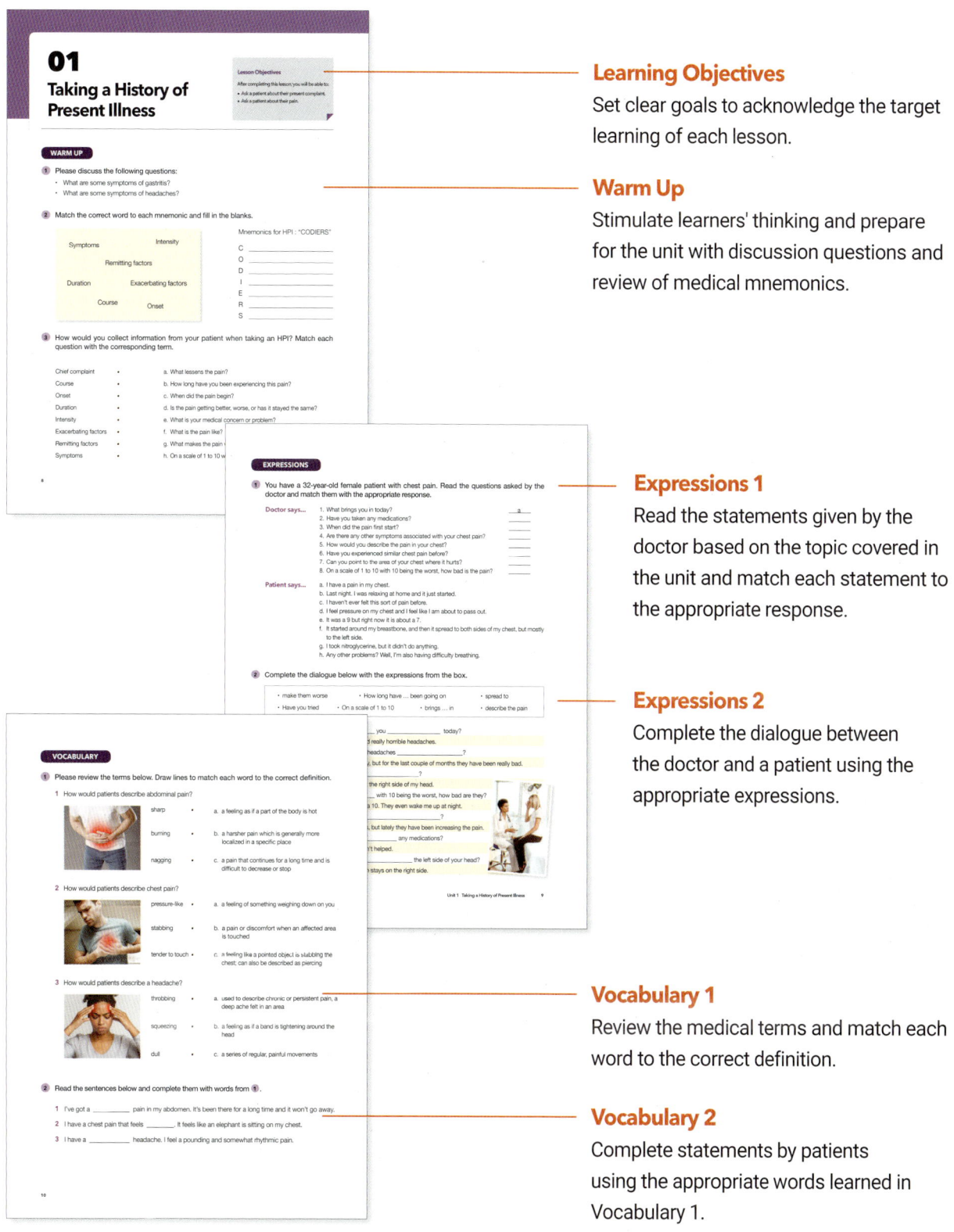

Learning Objectives
Set clear goals to acknowledge the target learning of each lesson.

Warm Up
Stimulate learners' thinking and prepare for the unit with discussion questions and review of medical mnemonics.

Expressions 1
Read the statements given by the doctor based on the topic covered in the unit and match each statement to the appropriate response.

Expressions 2
Complete the dialogue between the doctor and a patient using the appropriate expressions.

Vocabulary 1
Review the medical terms and match each word to the correct definition.

Vocabulary 2
Complete statements by patients using the appropriate words learned in Vocabulary 1.

Unit Composition

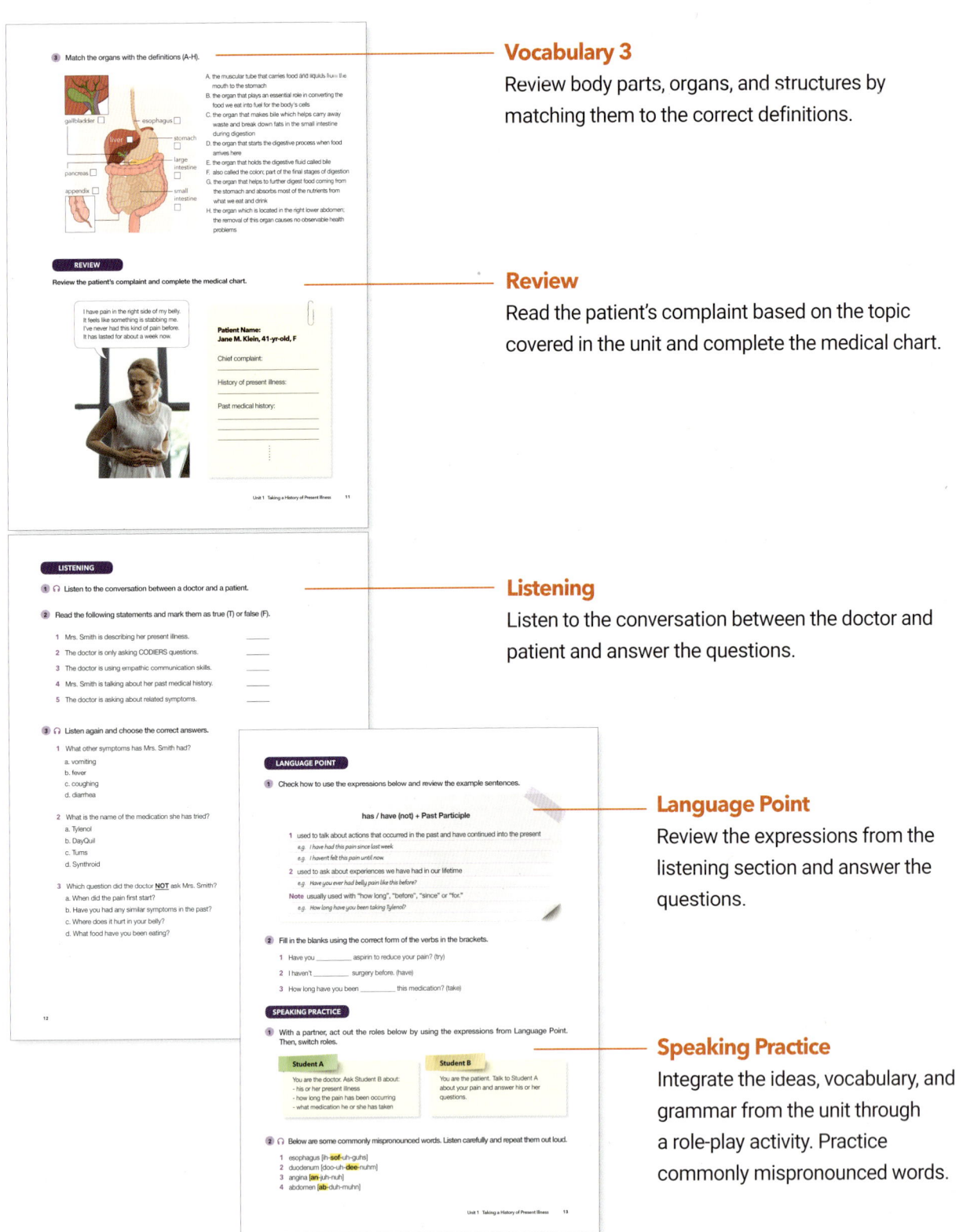

Vocabulary 3
Review body parts, organs, and structures by matching them to the correct definitions.

Review
Read the patient's complaint based on the topic covered in the unit and complete the medical chart.

Listening
Listen to the conversation between the doctor and patient and answer the questions.

Language Point
Review the expressions from the listening section and answer the questions.

Speaking Practice
Integrate the ideas, vocabulary, and grammar from the unit through a role-play activity. Practice commonly mispronounced words.

Table of Contents

	Unit Contents	Learning Objectives	Page
01	Taking a History of Present Illness	• Ask a patient about their present complaint. • Ask a patient about their pain.	8
02	Asking about Past Medical History, Medications, and Allergies	• Ask a patient about their past medical history. • Ask a patient about medications and allergies.	14
03	Taking Family History and Social History	• Ask a patient about their family history. • Ask a patient about their social history.	20
04	Taking Review of Systems	• Ask a patient about their review of systems.	26
05	Describing Vitals and Giving Instructions During Examination	• Explain a patient's vital signs to them. • Give instructions to a patient during a physical examination.	32
06	Explaining Physical Exam Findings & Clinical Impressions	• Explain physical exam findings to a patient. • Explain clinical impressions to a patient.	38
07	Discussing Labs and Imaging	• Discuss labs with a patient. • Discuss imaging with a patient.	44
08	Discussing Test Results and Diagnosis	• Discuss test results with a patient. • Discuss diagnosis with a patient.	50
09	Developing Empathic Communication Skills	• Better recognize patients' emotions. • Empathize with patients.	56
10	Describing Treatment Options	• Discuss treatment options with patients.	62
11	Educating Patients on Lifestyle Changes	• Educate patients on lifestyle modification. • Discuss the benefits of lifestyle modification.	68
12	Discussing Referrals and Admission	• Discuss referrals with patients. • Discuss admission arrangements with patients.	74
	Appendix	• Parts of the Body • Commonly Used Medical Terms • Answer Key • Listening Scripts	81

01
Taking a History of Present Illness

Lesson Objectives

After completing this lesson, you will be able to:
- Ask a patient about their present complaint.
- Ask a patient about their pain.

WARM UP

1. Please discuss the following questions:
   - What are some symptoms of gastritis?
   - What are some symptoms of headaches?

2. Match the correct word to each mnemonic and fill in the blanks.

   Symptoms   Intensity
   Remitting factors
   Duration   Exacerbating factors
   Course   Onset

   Mnemonics for HPI : "CODIERS"

   C _____
   O _____
   D _____
   I _____
   E _____
   R _____
   S _____

3. How would you collect information from your patient when taking an HPI? Match each question with the corresponding term.

Term		Question
Chief complaint	•	a. What lessens the pain?
Course	•	b. How long have you been experiencing this pain?
Onset	•	c. When did the pain begin?
Duration	•	d. Is the pain getting better, worse, or has it stayed the same?
Intensity	•	e. What is your medical concern or problem?
Exacerbating factors	•	f. What is the pain like?
Remitting factors	•	g. What makes the pain worse?
Symptoms	•	h. On a scale of 1 to 10 with 10 being the worst, how bad is the pain?

EXPRESSIONS

1 You have a 32-year-old female patient with chest pain. Read the questions asked by the doctor and match them with the appropriate response.

Doctor says…
1. What brings you in today? __a__
2. Have you taken any medications? ____
3. When did the pain first start? ____
4. Are there any other symptoms associated with your chest pain? ____
5. How would you describe the pain in your chest? ____
6. Have you experienced similar chest pain before? ____
7. Can you point to the area of your chest where it hurts? ____
8. On a scale of 1 to 10 with 10 being the worst, how bad is the pain? ____

Patient says…
a. I have a pain in my chest.
b. Last night. I was relaxing at home and it just started.
c. I haven't ever felt this sort of pain before.
d. I feel pressure on my chest and I feel like I am about to pass out.
e. It was a 9 but right now it is about a 7.
f. It started around my breastbone, and then it spread to both sides of my chest, but mostly to the left side.
g. I took nitroglycerine, but it didn't do anything.
h. Any other problems? Well, I'm also having difficulty breathing.

2 Complete the dialogue below with the expressions from the box.

• make them worse	• How long have … been going on	• spread to
• Have you tried	• On a scale of 1 to 10	• brings … in	• describe the pain

Doctor What __1_____ you _____ today?
Patient Well, doctor, lately I have had really horrible headaches.
Doctor __2_____ your headaches _____?
Patient I get headaches occasionally, but for the last couple of months they have been really bad.
Doctor Could you __3_____?
Patient Yes, it is a throbbing pain on the right side of my head.
Doctor __4_____ with 10 being the worst, how bad are they?
Patient It ranges between an 8 and a 10. They even wake me up at night.
Doctor Does anything __5_____?
Patient I like to take spinning classes, but lately they have been increasing the pain.
Doctor I see. __6_____ any medications?
Patient I've taken Tylenol, but it hasn't helped.
Doctor Do your headaches __7_____ the left side of your head?
Patient No, I don't think so. The pain stays on the right side.

VOCABULARY

1 Please review the terms below. Draw lines to match each word to the correct definition.

1 How would patients describe abdominal pain?

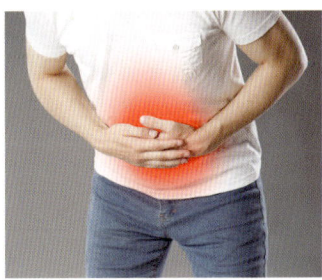

sharp • a. a feeling as if a part of the body is hot

burning • b. a harsher pain which is generally more localized in a specific place

nagging • c. a pain that continues for a long time and is difficult to decrease or stop

2 How would patients describe chest pain?

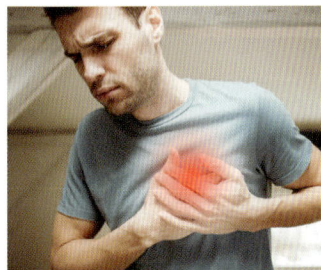

pressure-like • a. a feeling of something weighing down on you

stabbing • b. a pain or discomfort when an affected area is touched

tender to touch • c. a feeling like a pointed object is stabbing the chest; can also be described as piercing

3 How would patients describe a headache?

throbbing • a. used to describe chronic or persistent pain, a deep ache felt in an area

squeezing • b. a feeling as if a band is tightening around the head

dull • c. a series of regular, painful movements

2 Read the sentences below and complete them with words from **1**.

1 I've got a _____ pain in my abdomen. It's been there for a long time and it won't go away.

2 I have a chest pain that feels _____. It feels like an elephant is sitting on my chest.

3 I have a _____ headache. I feel a pounding and somewhat rhythmic pain.

3 Match the organs with the definitions (A-H).

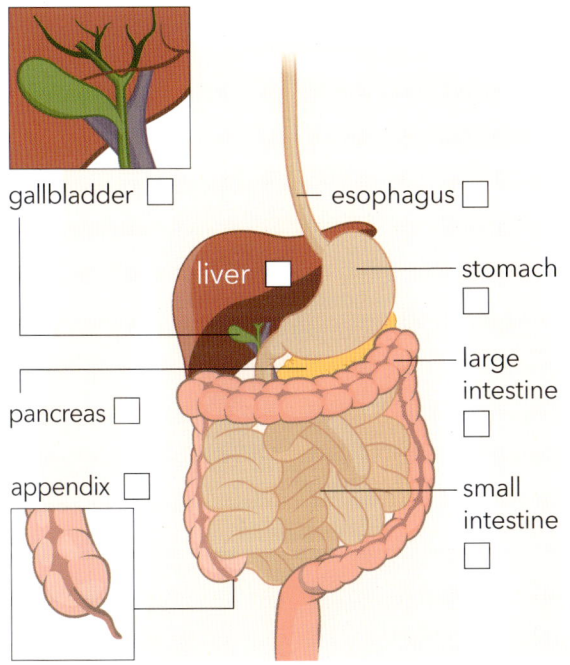

gallbladder ☐ esophagus ☐
liver ☐ stomach ☐
large intestine ☐
pancreas ☐
appendix ☐ small intestine ☐

A. the muscular tube that carries food and liquids from the mouth to the stomach
B. the organ that plays an essential role in converting the food we eat into fuel for the body's cells
C. the organ that makes bile which helps carry away waste and break down fats in the small intestine during digestion
D. the organ that starts the digestive process when food arrives here
E. the organ that holds the digestive fluid called bile
F. also called the colon; part of the final stages of digestion
G. the organ that helps to further digest food coming from the stomach and absorbs most of the nutrients from what we eat and drink
H. the organ which is located in the right lower abdomen; the removal of this organ causes no observable health problems

REVIEW

Review the patient's complaint and complete the medical chart.

I have pain in the right side of my belly. It feels like something is stabbing me. I've never had this kind of pain before. It has lasted for about a week now.

Patient Name:
Jane M. Klein, 41-yr-old, F

Chief complaint:
_____

History of present illness:
_____

Past medical history:
_____
_____
_____

LISTENING

1 🎧 Listen to the conversation between a doctor and a patient.

2 Read the following statements and mark them as true (T) or false (F).

1 Mrs. Smith is describing her present illness. _____
2 The doctor is only asking CODIERS questions. _____
3 The doctor is using empathic communication skills. _____
4 Mrs. Smith is talking about her past medical history. _____
5 The doctor is asking about related symptoms. _____

3 🎧 Listen again and choose the correct answers.

1 What other symptoms has Mrs. Smith had?
   a. vomiting
   b. fever
   c. coughing
   d. diarrhea

2 What is the name of the medication she has tried?
   a. Tylenol
   b. DayQuil
   c. Tums
   d. Synthroid

3 Which question does the doctor **NOT** ask Mrs. Smith?
   a. When did the pain first start?
   b. Have you had any similar symptoms in the past?
   c. Where does it hurt in your belly?
   d. What food have you been eating?

LANGUAGE POINT

1 Check how to use the expressions below and review the example sentences.

has / have (not) + Past Participle

1 used to talk about actions that occurred in the past and have continued into the present

e.g. *I have had this pain since last week.*

e.g. *I haven't felt this pain until now.*

2 used to ask about experiences we have had in our lifetime

e.g. *Have you ever had belly pain like this before?*

Note usually used with "how long", "before", "since" or "for."

e.g. *How long have you been taking Tylenol?*

2 Fill in the blanks using the correct form of the verbs in the brackets.

1 Have you _____ aspirin to reduce your pain? (try)

2 I haven't _____ surgery before. (have)

3 How long have you been _____ this medication? (take)

SPEAKING PRACTICE

1 With a partner, act out the roles below by using the expressions from Language Point. Then, switch roles.

Student A

You are the doctor. Ask Student B about:
- his or her present illness
- how long the pain has been occurring
- what medication he or she has taken

Student B

You are the patient. Talk to Student A about your pain and answer his or her questions.

2 🎧 Below are some commonly mispronounced words. Listen carefully and repeat them out loud.

1 esophagus [ih-**sof**-uh-guhs]
2 duodenum [doo-uh-**dee**-nuhm]
3 angina [**an**-juh-nuh]
4 abdomen [**ab**-duh-muhn]

02
Asking About Past Medical History, Medications, and Allergies

Lesson Objectives

After completing this lesson, you will be able to:
- Ask a patient about their past medical history.
- Ask a patient about medications and allergies.

WARM UP

1 Please discuss the following questions:
- What is the most common cause of myocardial infarction?
- What are the symptoms of hypertension?

2 Match the correct word to each mnemonic and fill in the blanks.

Signs / Symptoms

Allergies

Past pertinent medical history

Medications

Last menstrual cycle

Events leading up to present illness / injury

Mnemonics for PMH : "SAMPLE"

S _____
A _____
M _____
P _____
L _____
E _____

3 How would you collect information from your patient when taking a PMH? Match each question with the corresponding term.

Signs / Symptoms • a. What is your concern today?

Allergies • b. Do you have any allergies?

Medications • c. Are you on any medications?

Past pertinent medical history • d. Have you had any similar symptoms before?

Last menstrual cycle • e. When was your last period and was it normal?

Events leading up to present illness / injury • f. Is there anything else I should know that is related to your current condition?

EXPRESSIONS

1 You have a 24-year-old female patient who has had nausea for the last 12 hours. Read the questions asked by the doctor and match them with the appropriate response.

Doctor says...
1. Do you have any chronic illnesses such as heart disease, diabetes, asthma, bleeding disorder, etc.? _a_
2. Have you had any major or minor surgery before? ____
3. What was the outcome after the surgery? ____
4. Were there any complications from the surgery? ____
5. Are you currently taking any prescribed medications or over-the-counter drugs? ____
6. Please tell me why and how often you take the medications? ____
7. Does medication help you with your symptoms? ____
8. Do you have any allergies to medications? ____
9. Do you have any allergies to food, pets, or anything else? ____

Patient says...
a. I have hypertension and I was diagnosed with it about 10 years ago.
b. I take one tab of lisinopril daily for hypertension and also aspirin when I have a headache.
c. As far as I know, I have no allergies to medications.
d. The surgeries were successful and no more follow-ups were needed.
e. I had a minor infection on the appendix surgical site but it got better with antibiotics and daily wound care.
f. Yes. When I eat peanuts, I get rashes.
g. I had a tonsillectomy when I was a kid and my appendix was removed about 5 years ago.
h. I take lisinopril and aspirin.
i. Yes, my blood pressure is controlled with medication and aspirin reduces my pain.

2 Complete the dialogue below with the expressions from the box.

• Do you have	• currently taking	• Have you had
• the outcome	• work well to control	• I should know about

Doctor Do you have any past medical history __1_____?
Patient Yes, I have type 2 diabetes.
Doctor Are you __2_____ any prescribed medications or over-the-counter drugs?
Patient Yes, I take insulin, as needed, after checking my blood sugar level.
Doctor Does insulin __3_____ your blood sugar level?
Patient Yes, it keeps my levels within the normal range.
Doctor __4_____ any major or minor surgery before?
Patient I recently had knee surgery.
Doctor I see, what was __5_____ of that surgery?
Patient I can walk without pain now and my surgeon told me that the surgery was very successful.
Doctor __6_____ any allergies to medications, food, etc?
Patient Yes. If I take Claritin, I have difficulty breathing.

VOCABULARY

1 Please review the terms below. Draw lines to match each word to the correct definition.

1 How would patients describe their allergic reactions?

conjunctivitis •   a. a raised, itchy, red rash

allergic rhinitis •   b. itchy, red, watering eyes

hives •   c. sneezing and an itchy, runny, or blocked nose

2 How would patients describe their symptoms of hypertension?

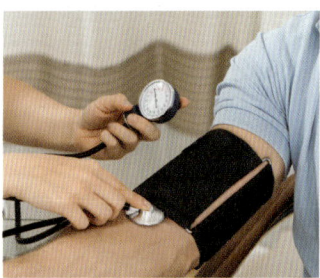

confusion •   a. an overall feeling of tiredness or lack of energy

fatigue •   b. having a fast-beating, fluttering, or pounding heart

palpitations •   c. a symptom that makes you feel as if you can't think clearly

3 How would patients describe their symptoms of a chest pain?

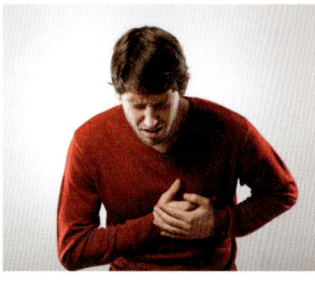

heartburn •   a. stomach discomfort and the sensation of wanting to vomit

indigestion •   b. a persistent or reoccurring pain or discomfort in the upper abdomen

nausea •   c. a burning sensation in the chest that often is accompanied by a bitter taste in the throat or mouth

2 Read the sentences below and complete them with words from **1**.

1 If I touch a cat, I get _____ on my skin.

2 I feel _____ in my chest. Should I go to a hospital?

3 I don't feel good. I have _____ and may throw up soon.

3 Match the vessels with the definitions (A-E).

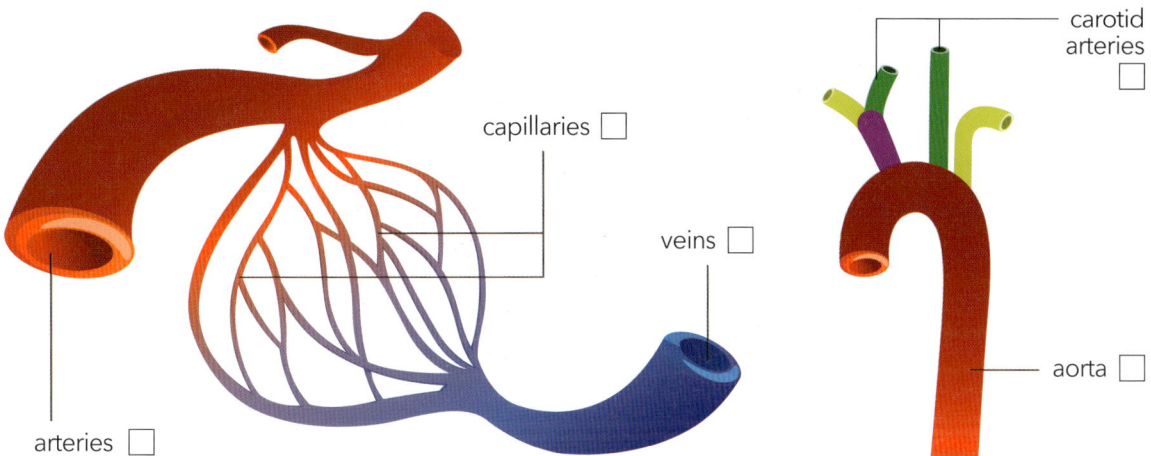

A. blood vessels that deliver oxygen-rich blood from the heart to tissues in the body
B. small blood vessels that connect arteries to veins
C. vessels that carry blood towards the heart
D. the largest artery in the heart
E. major blood vessels in the neck that supply blood to the brain, neck, and face

REVIEW

Review the patient's complaint and complete the medical chart.

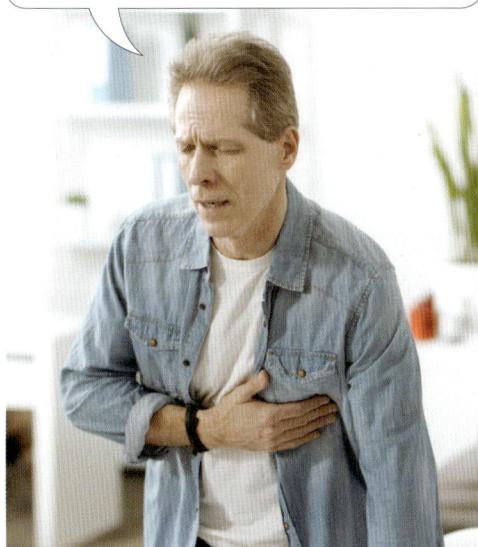

> My father has hypertension and I am currently having heart palpitations. I'm not taking any medications right now.

Patient Name:
David GIGLIOTTI, 48-yr-old, M

Chief complaint:
_____

Past medical history:
_____

Family history:
_____
_____
_____

Unit 2 Asking About Past Medical History, edications, and Allergies   17

LISTENING

1 🎧 Listen to the conversation between a doctor and a patient.

2 Read the following statements and mark them as true (T) or false (F).

1. Mr. Mansfield has a surgical history. _____
2. The doctor is asking if Mr. Mansfield is on any medications. _____
3. Mr. Mansfield can have a CT and an MRI without sedation. _____
4. Mr. Mansfield has pet allergies. _____
5. Mr. Mansfield sees his family doctor regularly. _____

3 🎧 Listen again and choose the correct answers.

1. Why did Mr. Mansfield get admitted to the hospital?
   a. chest pain
   b. knee pain
   c. appendicitis
   d. cancer

2. Which prescribed medication is Mr. Mansfield on?
   a. analgesics
   b. insulin
   c. blood thinner
   d. antibiotics

3. Which question does the doctor **NOT** ask Mr. Mansfield?
   a. Are you on any prescribed medications?
   b. How is your blood sugar level?
   c. Can you please tell me about your past medical history?
   d. Do you have allergic reactions to any medications?

LANGUAGE POINT

1 Check how to use the expressions below and review the example sentences.

1 Do you have any + diseases / symptoms + I should know about?

: used to check if a patient has a certain symptom or disease

e.g. *Do you have any allergies to food I should know about?*

2 I have + diseases / symptoms. (↔ I don't have any + diseases / symptoms.)

: used to tell a doctor about a certain disease or symptom

e.g. *I have palpitations.*   *e.g.* *I don't have any food allergies.*

3 Are you on any + medications?

: used to check if a patient is currently taking medication

e.g. *Are you on any medications for your high blood pressure?*

2 Circle the most appropriate word for each sentence.

1 Do you have (allergies / symptoms) to pets or food that I should know about?

2 I don't have any (food allergies / medication allergies). I can eat anything.

3 Are you on any (treatment / medications) for your rhinitis?

SPEAKING PRACTICE

1 With a partner, act out the roles below by using the expressions from Language Point. Then, switch roles.

Student A

You are the doctor. Ask Student B about:
- any past medical history or chronic illnesses
- any medications he or she is currently on
- any allergic reactions he or she has

Student B

You are the patient. Talk to Student A about your medical history and answer his or her questions.

2 Below are some commonly mispronounced words. Listen carefully and repeat them out loud.

1 arrhythmia [uh-**rith-**mee-uh]
2 atherosclerosis [ath-uh-roh-skluh-**roh**-sis]
3 fatigue [fuh-**teeg**]
4 atrium [**ey-**tree-uhm]

03
Taking Family History and Social History

Lesson Objectives

After completing this lesson, you will be able to:
- Ask a patient about their family history.
- Ask a patient about their social history.

WARM UP

1 Please discuss the following questions:
- How dangerous is cancer?
- What causes hyperlipidemia?

2 Match the correct word to each mnemonic and fill in the blanks.

Blood pressure (high)
Arthritis
Lung disease
Diabetes
Cancer
Heart disease
Alcoholism
Stroke
Mental health disorders

Mnemonics for FH : "BALD CHASM"

B _____
A _____
L _____
D _____
C _____
H _____
A _____
S _____
M _____

3 How would you gather information on your patients' family history? Match each question with the corresponding terms (more than one term will apply to each question).

- Blood pressure (high)
- Arthritis
- Lung disease
- Diabetes
- Cancer
- Heart disease
- Alcoholism
- Stroke
- Mental health disorders

a. Does anyone in your family have any long-term health problems like heart disease, diabetes, cancer, or lung disease?

b. Does anyone in your family have any health issues like high blood pressure, arthritis, or a history of strokes?

c. Does anyone in your family suffer from alcoholism or mental health disorders?

EXPRESSIONS

1 You have a 53-year-old female patient with breast lumps. Read the questions/statements given by the doctor and match them with the appropriate response.

Doctor says...
1. Does anyone in your family have any long-term health problems or any other health issues? _a_
2. Has anyone in your family been diagnosed with breast cancer or any other cancers? ____
3. How old was your mother when she was first diagnosed? ____
4. Is her cancer currently being treated or is it in remission? ____
5. Do you currently use any alcohol, tobacco, or other substances? ____
6. Do you have a lot of stress? ____
7. Thank you for sharing this information. ____

Patient says...
a. My father died when he was in his early 60s due to a stroke.
b. Well, I'm afraid that I have breast cancer. That definitely stresses me out.
c. She had chemotherapy and now only an annual checkup is needed.
d. I drink a little beer occasionally and that is it.
e. Yes, my mother had breast cancer.
f. I believe my mother was in her 50s.
g. No problem, doctor.

2 Complete the dialogue below with the expressions from the box.

• What's … like	• Have you checked	• any health issues like
• Would you please	• if you don't mind	• Do you use

Doctor __1_____ tell me if anyone in your family has any long-term health problems like heart disease, diabetes, kidney disease, or lung disease?

Patient No, all my family members are in good shape.

Doctor Does anyone in your family have __2_____ high blood pressure, high cholesterol, or asthma?

Patient Actually my father was diagnosed with high cholesterol but he's not taking any medications.

Doctor __3_____ your cholesterol level recently?

Patient Yes, I checked it this year during my annual check-up and it was normal.

Doctor That's very good. __4_____ any alcohol, tobacco, or illegal substances?

Patient Yes, I've been smoking cigarettes for 30 years.

Doctor I would like to talk about your daily life, __5_____. Who do you live with now?

Patient I'm not married and I live alone.

Doctor __6_____ your home life _____?

Patient I cook every day and make sure to keep the house clean. Other than that nothing special.

Doctor Is there anything else about your daily life you would like to share with me?

Patient I'm a bit depressed because I lost my job a few weeks ago.

VOCABULARY

1 Please review the terms below. Draw lines to match each word to the correct definition.

1 How would patients describe their symptoms of breast cancer?

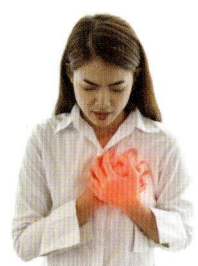

nipple retraction •   a. a mass of indefinite size and shape

lump •   b. the point of the breast turns inward

discharge •   c. any fluid or liquid that comes out of a nipple

2 How would patients describe their symptoms of blood cancer?

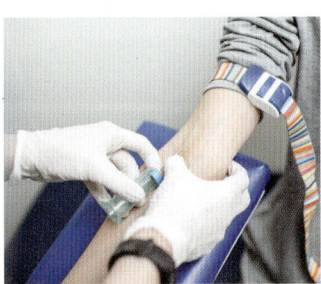

loss of appetite •   a. a feeling of coldness accompanied by shivering

night sweats •   b. repeated episodes of extreme perspiration that may soak the nightclothes or bedding

chills •   c. not having the same desire to eat as before

3 How would patients describe their symptoms of brain cancer?

blurred vision •   a. a loss of sharpness of eyesight, making objects appear out of focus and hazy

peripheral vision loss •   b. seeing a double image where there should only be one

double vision •   c. also known as tunnel vision; not being able to see objects unless they're right in front of you

2 Read the sentences below and complete them with words from **1**.

1 I don't know why but I have some _____ from my breast.

2 I have terrible _____, they wake me up in the middle of night.

3 What is happening to my eyes! I have _____. Everything is out of focus.

3 Match the tissues with the definitions (A-D).

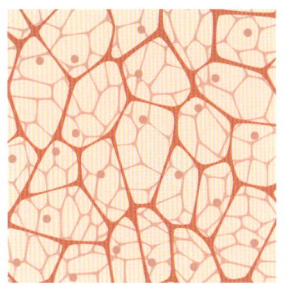 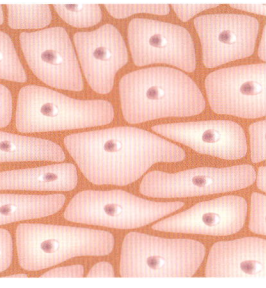 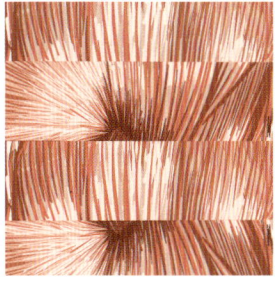 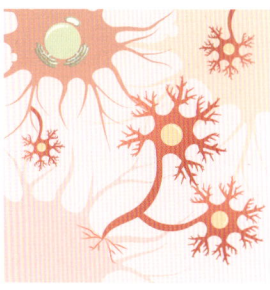

connective   epithelial   muscle   nervous

A. tissues that provide support, bind together, and protect other tissues and organs in the body
B. thin tissues that cover the exposed surfaces of the body
C. the only tissue in the body that has the ability to contract and therefore move the other parts of the body
D. tissue that monitors and regulates the functions of the body; found in the brain, spinal cord, and nerves

REVIEW

Review the patient's complaint and complete the medical chart.

> I live alone at home, I don't drink any alcohol, and I don't feel like I'm stressed.
> All my family members are healthy.

Patient Name:
Maria CECIL, 28yr-old, F

Chief complaint:
palpable lumps on R breast

History of present illness: no pain, no discharge, no other complaints

Past medical history: no PMH

Family history:
_____

Social history:
_____

LISTENING

1 🎧 Listen to the conversation between a doctor and a patient.

2 Read the following statements and mark them as true (T) or false (F).

1. Mr. Boggs's family members do not have any medical history. _____
2. The doctor is asking if Mr. Boggs uses any illegal substances. _____
3. Mr. Boggs has lots of stress at home. _____
4. The doctor is asking about social history. _____
5. Mr. Boggs lives alone at home. _____

3 🎧 Listen again and choose the correct answers.

1. Which medical condition did the grandfather have?
   a. dementia
   b. stroke
   c. arthritis
   d. cataract

2. Which substance does Mr. Boggs use?
   a. alcohol
   b. tobacco
   c. street drugs
   d. none

3. Which question does the doctor **NOT** ask Mr. Boggs?
   a. Does anyone in your family have any medical issues?
   b. What's your home life like?
   c. Do you have any stress at home?
   d. Where is your house located?

LANGUAGE POINT

1 Check how to use the expressions below and read the example sentences.

1 What's your + Noun + like?

: used to ask about a patient's daily routine, habits, and other personal lifestyle information

e.g. What's your sleeping pattern like?

e.g. What's your family like? Can you get any support if you get ill?

2 How is + Noun?

: used to continue getting information from a patient

e.g. So, you try to keep a balanced lifestyle. How is your diet?

e.g. I see you're happy at home. How is your job?

2 Circle the most appropriate word for each sentence.

1. (What / How) is your drinking habit? Do you still binge drink?
2. I see you go to the gym regularly. How is your (diet / smoking)? Do you keep it balanced?
3. What's your (house / work) like? Do any of your co-workers cause you any trouble?

SPEAKING PRACTICE

1 With a partner, act out the roles below by using the expressions from Language Point. Then, switch roles.

Student A

You are the doctor. Ask Student B about:
- his or her family medical history
- any alcohol, tobacco, or illegal substance use
- daily life at home and any stress

Student B

You are the patient. Talk to Student A about your history and answer his or her questions.

2 Below are some commonly mispronounced words. Listen carefully and repeat them out loud.

1. benign tumor [bih-**nahyn too**-mer]
2. chemotherapy [kee-moh-**ther**-uh-pee]
3. melanoma [mel-uh-**noh**-muh]
4. leukemia [loo-**kee**-mee-uh]

04
Taking Review of Systems

Lesson Objectives

After completing this lesson, you will be able to:
- Ask a patient about their review of systems.

WARM UP

1 Please discuss the following questions:
- What causes a herniated disc?
- What would be treatment options for severe back pain?

2 Match the correct word to each mnemonic and fill in the blanks.

Respiratory   Urinary
Nervous
Muscular   Reproductive
Lymphatic   Skeletal
Digestive   Integumentary
Cardiovascular   Endocrine

Mnemonics for FH : "RUN MRS. LIDEC"

R _____   L _____
U _____   I _____
N _____   D _____
M _____   E _____
R _____   C _____
S _____

3 How would you collect information from your patient when taking an ROS? Match each term to the appropriate question.

Respiratory • a. Do you have a headache, any dizziness, or have you recently experienced a loss of consciousness?
Urinary • b. Are you having any difficulty with urination?
Nervous • c. Do you currently have a cough or shortness of breath?
Muscular • d. Are you having any joint or muscle pain?
Reproductive • e. Do you have any vaginal bleeding, and what's your menstrual cycle duration and frequency?
Skeletal • f. Do you have any skin problems, wounds, or rashes?
Lymphatic • g. Do you have any swelling in your lymph nodes?
Integumentary • h. Do you have any back pain or major orthopedic injuries?
Digestive • i. Do you have any chest pain, irregular heartbeats, or hypertension?
Endocrine • j. Do you have diabetes or have you noticed a change in weight recently?
Cardiovascular • k. Do you have any nausea, vomiting, diarrhea, or constipation?

EXPRESSIONS

1 You have a 65-year-old male patient with severe back pain. Read the questions asked by the doctor and match them with the appropriate response.

Doctor says...
1. Do you have any difficulty breathing? _a_
2. How's your urination? _____
3. Do you have a headache now? _____
4. Do you have nausea, vomiting, or diarrhea? _____
5. Do you have diabetes or have you experienced any recent changes in your weight? _____
6. Are you experiencing any chest pain or discomfort right now? _____
7. Do you have any other pain besides your back? _____

Patient says...
a. Yes, I have difficulty breathing when my back is hurting.
b. I lost 3kg in the past 2 months.
c. No, I only have the back pain and I can't bear it anymore.
d. Yes, the nausea is on and off.
e. No problem with urination.
f. No, nothing like that.
g. I don't have one right now.

2 Complete the dialogue below with the expressions from the box.

| • check … thoroughly | • empty your bladder | • anything abnormal |
| • Have you noticed | • any difficulty breathing | • do you feel any | • been diagnosed with |

Doctor Now I would like to _1_____ all your body systems _____. If you have any questions, you can ask me anytime.

Patient Sure, I will do that.

Doctor First, _2_____ headaches or dizziness, or have you noticed any vision changes?

Patient I get a headache once in a while but no pain right now.

Doctor When did you _3_____ last, and did you experience any discomfort?

Patient I went to the bathroom this morning and there was nothing unusual.

Doctor _4_____ any nausea recently?

Patient I vomited once, right after I ate breakfast this morning.

Doctor How is your menstrual cycle? When was your last period and was there _5_____?

Patient No, doctor. My cycle is regular and everything was normal.

Doctor How is your breathing right now? Are you experiencing _6_____?

Patient No, I'm absolutely fine.

Doctor Do you have any chest discomfort, pain or palpitations?

Patient Yes, I think I may be having some palpitations.

Doctor Have you _7_____ diabetes or had any recent weight changes?

Patient I don't have diabetes and I haven't noticed any weight changes.

VOCABULARY

1 Please review the terms below. Draw lines to match each word to the correct definition.

1 How would patients describe their symptoms of a herniated disc?

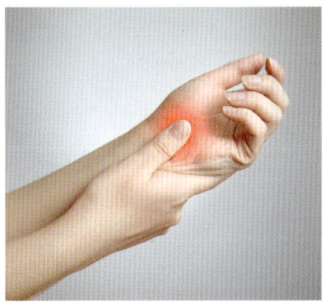

burning sensation •   a. an abnormal sensation that can occur anywhere in the body, but mostly felt in the fingers, hands, feet, and/or arms

aching sensation •   b. muscle pain that affects a small part of the body, usually caused by overuse

tingling sensation •   c. a sharp, prickly pain that feels like heat or pins and needles

2 How would patients describe their symptoms of back pain?

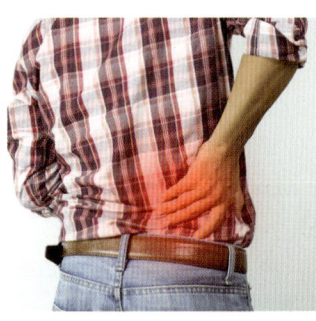

shooting pain •   a. most often related to tension, overuse, or muscle injury from exercise or hard physical labor

muscle ache •   b. often described as an electrical sensation accompanied by sharp pain

weakness •   c. pain that happens when your full effort doesn't produce a normal muscle contraction or movement

3 How would patients describe their symptoms of back pain?

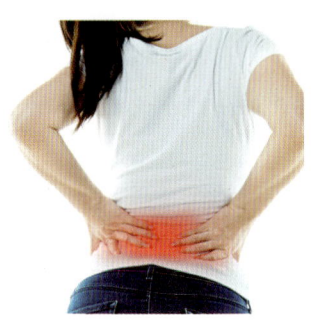

acute •   a. a pain that can be mild and last for just a moment, or it might be severe and last for weeks or months

intermittent •   b. a pain that lasts at least 12 weeks; it may feel sharp or dull, causing a burning or aching sensation in the affected areas

chronic •   c. a pain that comes and goes without any apparent reason

2 Read the sentences below and complete them with words from **1**.

1 I feel _____ sensations in my left hand and foot. It feels prickly and hot.

2 I have a _____ pain down my back and it feels almost electric.

3 Doctor, I cannot sleep well at night due to _____ back pain. I've had this pain for 1 year.

1 Match the structures with the definitions (A-E).

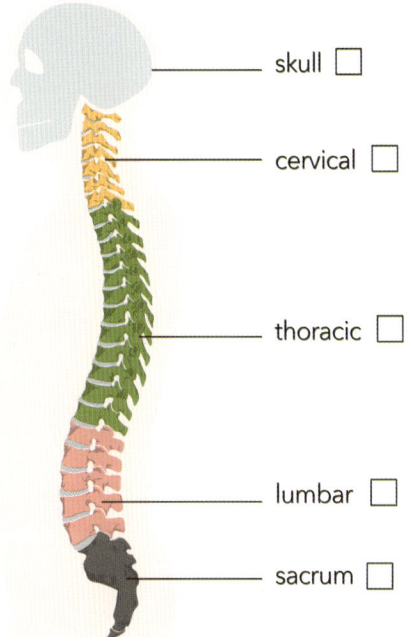

- skull ☐
- cervical ☐
- thoracic ☐
- lumbar ☐
- sacrum ☐

A. a framework of bone or cartilage that provides structure to the head and face while also protecting the brain

B. bones that bear the weight of the body

C. bones that hold the rib cage which protect the heart and lungs

D. bones that support and promote the movement of the head and neck

E. bones that connect the spine to the hip bones

REVIEW

Review the patient's complaint and complete the medical chart.

I have a burning sensation in my back.
I'm not having difficulty breathing, there is no chest discomfort, and there are no other symptoms.

Patient Name:
Kim GREEN , 56-yr-old, F

Chief complaint:
_____

Past medical history:
Pneumonia at age 51

Family history:
father has arthritis

Review of systems:
_____
_____

LISTENING

1 🎧 Listen to the conversation between a doctor and a patient.

2 Read the following statements and mark them as true (T) or false (F).

1. The doctor finished taking family and social history from the patient. _____
2. The doctor is asking necessary questions using **"RUN MRS. LIDEC"**. _____
3. The patient is a female. _____
4. The patient has a surgical wound on their chest. _____
5. The doctor asked about the patient's cardiac system. _____

3 🎧 Listen again and choose the correct answers.

1. What sensation does the patient have in their left hand?
   a. numbness
   b. shooting
   c. weakness
   d. tingling

2. Which respiratory symptoms is the patient experiencing?
   a. shortness of breath
   b. cough
   c. sputum
   d. none

3. Which system is abnormal?
   a. digestive
   b. lymphatic
   c. nervous
   d. urinary

LANGUAGE POINT

1 Check how to use the expressions below and read the example sentences.

1 Do you feel + body parts + Gerund ?

: used to ask about symptoms in detail, add a verb in the gerund form after body parts

e.g. Do you feel your throat swelling?   e.g. Do you feel your face getting hot?

2 Do / Does your + body parts + feel + Adjective ?

: used to ask about symptoms in detail, add an adjective to the end

e.g. Does your back feel uncomfortable?   e.g. Do your legs or arms feel numb?

Note Both expressions are used for the same purpose, however, expression 1 is used to describe the pain or symptom with verbs while 2 is used to describe the pain or symptoms with adjectives.

2 Circle the most appropriate word for each sentence.

1. Does your ear feel (stuffed / stuffy)?
2. Do you feel your stomach (bloating / to bloat)?
3. Do your fingers feel (tingly / tingle)?

SPEAKING PRACTICE

1 With a partner, act out the roles below by using the expressions from Language Point. Then, switch roles.

Student A

You are the doctor. Ask Student B about:
- any respiratory, cardiac, urinary, or skeletal symptoms
- any nervous, muscular, or reproductive symptoms
- any lymphatic, endocrine, or digestive symptoms

Student B

You are the patient. Talk to Student A about your concerns regarding your symptoms.

2 🎧 Below are some commonly mispronounced words. Listen carefully and repeat them out loud.

1. thoracic [thaw-**ras**-ik]
2. vertebra [**vur**-tuh-bruh]
3. sacrum [**sak**-ruhm], [**sey**-kruhm]
4. coccyx [**kok**-siks]

05
Describing Vitals and Giving Instructions During Examination

Lesson Objectives

After completing this lesson, you will be able to:
- Explain a patient's vital signs to them.
- Give instructions to a patient during a physical examination.

WARM UP

1 Please discuss the following questions:
- What are the 5 warning signs of a stroke?
- What temperature is fatal to humans?

2 Match the correct word to each mnemonic and fill in the blanks.

Inspection

Palpation

Percussion

Auscultation

Mnemonics for Physical examination:
"I Palpate People's Abdomens"

I _____
P _____
P _____
A _____

3 How would you collect information from your patient when completing a physical examination? Match each term to the corresponding question/statement.

Inspection •   a. How are you feeling today? (Generally, look for the patient's symptoms while the patient is talking.)

Palpation •   b. Please lie still while I tap on your abdomen.

Percussion •   c. Please lie down on the bed so I can check your abdomen. (Gently examine and watch the patient's face for signs of discomfort.)

Auscultation • d. Take a deep breath, in and out.

EXPRESSIONS

1 You have a 22-year-old male patient with a high fever. Read the questions/statements given by the nurse and match them with the appropriate response.

Nurse says...
1. Hi, Mr. Jones. How are you today? I'm Sue, one of the nurses here, and I am going to take your vitals.   __a__
2. I will be taking your blood pressure and pulse, so please remain silent.   ____
3. It's 140 over 90. Are you on any blood pressure medications?   ____
4. It should be around 120 over 80.   ____
5. Yes, perhaps. Now, I'm going to take your temperature.   ____
6. Yes, it's 39°C. Did you take any medications before you came to the hospital today?   ____
7. Your other vitals are normal except for the temperature. The doctor will be in shortly to discuss your blood pressure with you.   ____

Patient says...
a. Hi, Sue. I'm fine.
b. Thank you, Sue. I will wait for the doctor.
c. No, I don't take any medication. What's the normal range?
d. Yes, I took Tylenol but it didn't lower my fever.
e. I do think I may have a fever.
f. Oh I see, maybe it is high because I'm a little stressed right now.
g. OK. I will.

2 Complete the dialogue below with the expressions from the box.

• may need to	• take a deep ..... in and out	• Let's check
• Let me	• It should be	• it seems
		• shortness of breath

Doctor Hi Mr. Jones, I'm Dr. Lewis and __1_____ you have a fever today. How are you feeling?
Patient I'm doing fine, doctor. The nurse told me that my temperature is about 39 °C.
Doctor Right. __2_____ listen to your lungs first.
Patient OK. I'm ready.
Doctor Please __3_____ breath _____.
I can hear some abnormal sounds in your lungs. Have you been coughing lately?
Patient Yes. I started coughing about a week ago.
Doctor OK. __4_____ your oxygen level. This probe on your finger will measure your oxygen level.
Patient What's the normal level?
Doctor __5_____ above 94% and yours is at 92%. Do you feel any __6_____?
Patient When I walk up stairs, I guess I do have some difficulty breathing.
Doctor OK, Mr. Jones. You __7_____ get an X-ray to see if there is a lung infection.

Unit 5 Describing Vitals and Giving Instructions During Examination   33

VOCABULARY

1 Please review the terms below. Draw lines to match each word to the correct definition.

1 How would patients describe their symptoms of a stroke?

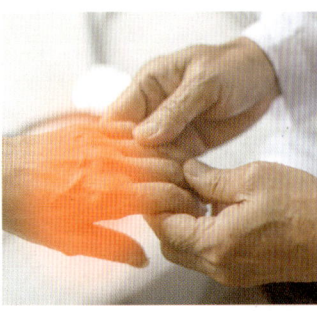

tingling • a. having no feeling in a specific part of one's body

numbness • b. experiencing a slight prickling or stinging sensation

tremor • c. an unintentional and uncontrollable rhythmic movement of a part or a limb of one's body

2 How would patients describe their symptoms of a stroke?

confusion • a. a symptom of being uncertain about what to do or being unable to understand something clearly

disoriented • b. a symptom characterized by poor pronunciation of words, mumbling, and/or a change in speed or rhythm while talking

slurred speech • c. having lost one's sense of time, place, or identity

3 How would patients describe their symptoms of a high fever?

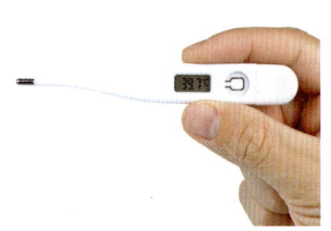

dehydration • a. an involuntary, temporary reddening of the skin, usually on the face

shivering • b. an involuntary or uncontrollable movement of the body

skin flushing • c. a symptom that occurs when the body loses more fluid than it can consume

2 Read the sentences below and complete them with words from **1**.

1 I have _____ in my left hand and I cannot feel anything.

2 My father suddenly became _____. Should I take him to an emergency room?

3 Doctor, I have a temp over 39.8 and uncontrollable _____. Can you see how badly I'm shaking now?

3 Match the structures with the definitions (A-F).

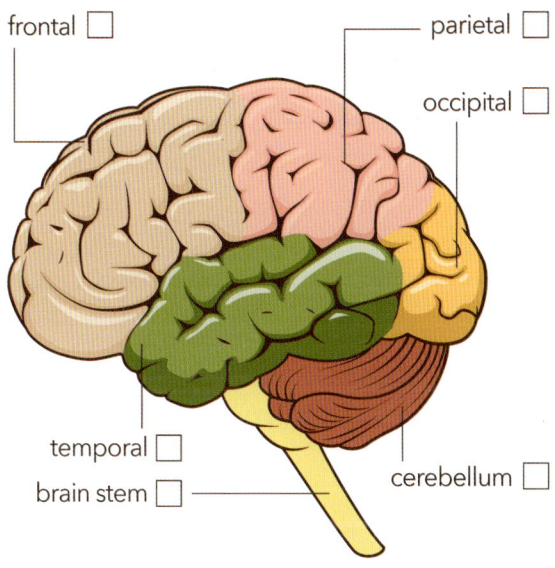

frontal ☐
parietal ☐
occipital ☐
temporal ☐
brain stem ☐
cerebellum ☐

A. stem that coordinates motor control signals sent from the brain to the body, and regulates vital cardiac and respiratory systems
B. lobe that is responsible for processing visual information from the eyes
C. part of the brain that helps process the senses of touch and pain
D. structure that plays a vital role in virtually all physical movement
E. lobe that controls important cognitive skills in humans such as emotional expression, problem solving, memory, language, judgment, and sexual behaviors
F. lobe that is involved with memory and hearing; processes information from our senses of smell, taste, and sound; plays a role in memory storage

REVIEW

Review the patient's complaint and complete the medical chart.

This morning I suddenly started to have slurred speech. I also feel some weakness in my right arm and leg.

Patient Name:
Sophie URIEGAS, 61-yr-old, F

Chief complaint:
_____

Past medical history:
nephrectomy at age 56

Family history:
Mother died from a stroke at age 82.

Review of systems:
_____
_____

LISTENING

1 🎧 Listen to the conversation a patient is having with a nurse and a doctor.

2 Read the following statements and mark them as true (T) or false (F).

1. The nurse is taking vitals including blood pressure and body temperature. _____
2. Ms. Lopez is not worried about her condition. _____
3. The doctor is giving instructions during the physical examinations. _____
4. The doctor will order further tests. _____
5. The left side of Ms. Lopez's body is weak. _____

3 🎧 Listen again and choose the correct answers.

1. What is Ms. Lopez's normal blood pressure?
   a. hypertensive
   b. hypotensive
   c. within the normal range (120/80)
   d. The doctor did not check her blood pressure level.

2. Which physical examination does the doctor **NOT** do?
   a. raising arms
   b. squeezing fingers
   c. numbness of body
   d. balance check

3. Which medical condition does the doctor want to rule out?
   a. heart attack
   b. stroke
   c. pneumonia
   d. otitis media

LANGUAGE POINT

1 Check how to use the expressions below and read the example sentences.

1 Can you + Verb ?
   e.g. *Can you bend your knees?*
   e.g. *Can you take a deep breath for me?*

2 Will you + Verb ?
   e.g. *Will you open your mouth and say "ah"?*
   e.g. *Will you move your wrists around in a circular motion?*

Note Both expressions are used to ask a patient to do certain actions for an examination. "Can" and "will" are both modals. Modals must be followed by infinitive verbs.

2 Circle the most appropriate word for each question below.

1 Can you (extend / extended) your legs?
2 Can you (squeeze / squeezing) my hands as hard as you can?
3 Will you (roll up / rolled up) your sleeve please?

SPEAKING PRACTICE

1 With a partner, act out the roles below by using the expressions from Language Point. Then, switch roles.

Student A
You are the doctor. Instruct Student B about:
- how to check vital signs
- how to breathe during a lung examination
- normal vital signs and findings

Student B
You are the patient. Talk to Student A about your concerns regarding vital signs.

2 Below are some commonly mispronounced words. Listen carefully and repeat them out loud.

1 paralysis [puh-**ral**-uh-sis]
2 ischemic [ih-**skee**-mik], [ih-**skem**-ik]
3 hemorrhagic [hem-uh-**raj**-ik]
4 aneurysm [**an**-yuh-riz-uhm]

06
Explaining Physical Exam Findings & Clinical Impressions

Lesson objectives

After completing this lesson, you will be able to:
- Explain physical exam findings to a patient.
- Explain clinical impressions to a patient.

WARM UP

1 Please discuss the following questions:
- What are the early signs of diabetes?
- Who is at high risk for diabetes?

2 Match the correct word to each mnemonic and fill in the blanks.

Subjective

Objective

Assessment

Plan

Mnemonics for organizing patient information : "SOAP"

S _____
O _____
A _____
P _____

3 Here are some words used for organizing patient information. Match each word with the corresponding definition.

Subjective •   a. This refers to observations that are verbally expressed by the patient, such as information about symptoms.

Objective •   b. It may involve ordering additional tests to rule out or confirm a diagnosis. It may also include prescribed treatment, such as medication or surgery.

Assessment •   c. It is the diagnosis or condition the patient is presenting with. There may be one clear diagnosis or a patient may have several issues. If a definitive diagnosis has not yet been made, then one possible diagnosis should be included.

Plan •   d. This involves observations that can be measured (vital signs, results of diagnostic tests, etc.), seen, heard, felt, or smelled.

EXPRESSIONS

1 You have a 33-year-old male patient with fatigue and weight loss. Read the statements given by the doctor and match them with the appropriate response.

Doctor says...
1. OK, Mr. Lee, here are the results from your physical exam. __a__
2. Your symptoms of fatigue and weight loss can be caused by a lot of things. ____
3. But I'm a little concerned about your frequent urination and increased thirst. ____
4. It's too early to diagnose but we should check for diabetes. ____
5. To confirm the exact diagnosis, I will order some blood tests to check your blood sugar level. ____
6. You will need to fast for 8 hours before the test, so you must come back tomorrow morning. ____

Patient says...
a. Yes, I'm listening.
b. Oh, I am worried about that because both of my parents have diabetes.
c. OK. I'll be here.
d. Oh, I was wondering about the reason for my recent weight loss.
e. When should I come back for the test?
f. Why do you think I go to the bathroom so often?

2 Complete the dialogue below with the expressions from the box.

• observe your symptoms	• quite normal	• you're going to	• prescribe you
• make sure	• would like to	• send you for	• If you experience

Doctor I think I have all the necessary information needed about this morning's accident involving a hit to your head. I __1_____ discuss my findings and recommendations with you.
Patient Of course, doctor. I'm ready.
Doctor Most of the physical exam findings are __2_____.
Patient Oh, that's really good to hear.
Doctor However, __3_____ need a few stitches on your head.
Patient Oh, I see. Can I go home after you stitch me up?
Doctor Well, I believe you might have a minor concussion so I want to __4_____ an x-ray.
Patient Why do I need an X-ray?
Doctor It's just a precaution. I want to __5_____ there is no fracture.
Patient I understand.
Doctor If the X-ray is normal, then you can go home and __6_____ there.
Patient OK. I hope it won't show anything serious.
Doctor I'm going to __7_____ some pain medication as well.
Patient Thank you, doctor.
Doctor __8_____ any new symptoms or a change in symptoms, you must come to my clinic right away.
Patient OK. I will closely monitor myself at home.

VOCABULARY

1 Please review the terms below. Draw lines to match each word to the correct definition.

1 How would patients describe their symptoms of diabetes?

frequent urination • a. an excessive, unquenchable desire to consume liquids

increased thirst • b. the strong, sudden need to relieve oneself, that occurs more than normal

extreme hunger • c. described as a constant or very frequent hunger

2 How would patients describe their symptoms of diabetes?

slow-healing sores • a. an overall feeling of tiredness or lack of energy

irritability • b. being likely to become frustrated or upset easily

fatigue • c. wounds that heal too slowly or incompletely, often producing abnormal scarring

3 How would patients describe their symptoms of a concussion?

drowsiness • a. feeling abnormally sleepy or tired during the day

seeing stars • b. a symptom that makes one feel as if one cannot think clearly

confusion • c. seeing flashes of light that occur in one's field of vision, which may look like fireworks, lightning bolts, or camera flashes

2 Read the sentences below and complete them with words from **1**.

1 I started having this _____. I have to drink about 1 liter of water every hour.

2 I'm concerned about my _____. They aren't fully healed and it has been more than 2 months.

3 As soon as I hit my head, I began _____. They were like camera flashes.

3 Match the major long-term diabetes complications with the definitions (A-F).

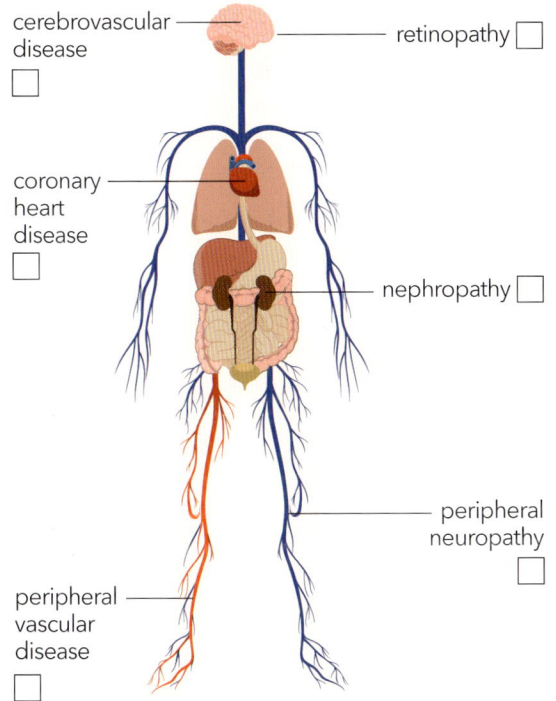

- cerebrovascular disease ☐
- coronary heart disease ☐
- peripheral vascular disease ☐
- retinopathy ☐
- nephropathy ☐
- peripheral neuropathy ☐

A. any damage to the retinas that can cause vision loss and blindness

B. a disease that causes restricted blood flow to the arms, legs, or other body parts and might cause potential loss of limbs

C. a disease of the kidneys caused by damage to the small blood vessels or to the units in the kidneys that clean the blood

D. narrowing or blockage of the coronary arteries causing a reduction of blood flow to the heart muscle

E. damage or dysfunction of one or more nerves that typically results in numbness, tingling, muscle weakness, and/or pain in the affected area

F. a condition that temporarily or permanently limits or blocks blood flow to the brain

REVIEW

Review the patient's complaint and complete the medical chart.

"I am experiencing fatigue and frequent urination. I have hypertension and my father was diagnosed with diabetes at age 43."

**Patient Name:
Mario SIMPSON, 51-yr-old, M**

Chief complaint:
_____

Present illness: no associated fever, no painful urination

Past medical history:
_____

Family history:
_____

Social history: Currently not consuming alcohol

⋮

Unit 6 Explaining Physical Exam Findings & Clinical Impressions

LISTENING

1 🎧 Listen to the conversation between a doctor and a patient.

2 Read the following statements and mark them as true (T) or false (F).

1. Mr. Greene visited the clinic due to a concern about diabetes-related symptoms. _____
2. The doctor is concerned about Mr. Greene's elevated blood sugar level. _____
3. Mr. Greene has a family history of diabetes. _____
4. The doctor will prescribe medications for diabetes today. _____
5. Mr. Greene doesn't have a follow-up appointment. _____

3 🎧 Listen again and choose the correct answers.

1. During the consultation, which symptom does the doctor **NOT** mention in regards to a possible diabetes diagnosis?
   a. recent weight loss
   b. extreme thirst
   c. frequent urination
   d. extreme hunger

2. Which treatment(s) will the doctor proceed with today? Select all correct answers.
   a. further lab test
   b. wound cleaning
   c. prescribe medication for diabetes
   d. prescribe antibiotics

3. Select one issue that the doctor is **NOT** currently worried about.
   a. elevated blood sugar level
   b. patient's diet
   c. patient's living style
   d. patient's allergic reactions

LANGUAGE POINT

1 Check how to use the expressions below and read the example sentences.

If + Subject + Verb (Simple Present Tense), Subject + will + Verb.

: used to inform a patient of next steps if/when they experience a certain symptom or pain

e.g. If your symptoms change during the night, you will need to visit the hospital right away.

e.g. If the X-ray results show a fracture, I will put a cast on your arm.

↔ **If + Subject + Verb (Simple Present Tense), Subject + will not (won't) + Verb.**

: the opposite form of the expression above

e.g. If your fever goes down tomorrow, I won't prescribe you any more medication.

e.g. If all the test results are within the normal range, you will be discharged.

2 Circle the most appropriate word for each sentence.

1. If you feel any further pain, I (will / won't) prescribe you more pain relievers.
2. If your symptoms get better, you (will / won't) need to visit me again.
3. If your blood pressure (will go / goes) down, I will send you for further CT scan.

SPEAKING PRACTICE

1 With a partner, act out the roles below by using the expressions from Language Point. Then, switch roles.

Student A
You are the doctor. Explain to Student B about:
- physical examination findings
- clinical impressions

Student B
You are the patient. Talk to Student A about your concerns regarding findings and impressions.

2 🎧 Below are some commonly mispronounced words. Listen carefully and repeat them out loud.

1. diabetes mellitus [dahy-uh-**bee**-tees **mel**-i-tuhs], [dahy-uh-bee-tees muh-**lahy**-tuhs]
2. ketoacidosis [ke-to-asi-**do**-sis]
3. diabetes insipidus [dahy-uh-**bee**-tees in-**sip**-i-duhs]
4. neuropathy [noo-**rop**-uh-thee]

07
Discussing Labs and Imaging

Lesson objectives

After completing this lesson, you will be able to:
- Discuss labs with a patient.
- Discuss imaging with a patient.

WARM UP

1 Please discuss the following questions:
- What are some recommended tests to confirm pneumonia?
- When do patients need to be admitted due to pneumonia?

2 Match the correct word to each mnemonic and fill in the blanks.

> Vascular   Infections
> Neoplastic
> Degenerative
> Intoxication
> Congenital
> Auto-immune
> Traumatic
> Endocrine (metabolic)

Mnemonics to eliminate incorrect assumptions : "VINDICATE"

V _____
I _____
N _____
D _____
I _____
C _____
A _____
T _____
E _____

3 Here are some possible causes of a patient's current symptoms. Match each word with the corresponding definition.

Vascular	•	a. relating to blood vessels
Infections	•	b. something present at birth but not necessarily inherited from the parents
Neoplastic	•	c. an abnormal growth of cells, also known as a tumor
Degenerative	•	d. a condition in which the immune system mistakenly attacks the body
Intoxication	•	e. a condition associated with drinking too much alcohol in a short amount of time
Congenital	•	f. a disease caused by germs or bacteria
Auto-immune	•	g. a disease or condition that gets worse as time progresses
Traumatic	•	h. relating to, or produced by, a trauma or wound
Endocrine (metabolic)	•	i. relating to, or deriving from, the metabolism of a living organism

EXPRESSIONS

1 You have a 56-year-old male patient with a productive cough. Read the questions/statements given by the doctor and match them with the appropriate response.

Doctor says...
1. I would like to send you for a chest X-ray first to see if there are any infections. __d__
2. Yes. I want to double check to make sure there is no infection in your lungs. _____
3. Yes, I will also order a basic blood test to see if there are any abnormalities. _____
4. After checking the results of the tests, you may need to be admitted for a couple of days. _____
5. We can discuss it all after reviewing the results, alright? _____
6. The nurse will assist you with an X-ray and blood test shortly. _____

Patient says...
a. I hope I can go home after the tests.
b. Are there any other tests you want to do besides the X-ray?
c. Oh, I see. I hope you don't find anything serious.
d. Is that really necessary?
e. OK. Where should I go now?
f. Thank you, doctor.

2 Complete the dialogue below with the expressions from the box.

• order … tests	• which may be causing	• by a lot of different reasons	• with further tests
• in a little bit	• take too long	• can show us	• concerned about

Doctor OK, Mr. Hasan, I'm __1_____ your chest pain, so I want to run some tests.
Patient Do you think it is something serious?
Doctor That's what we want to find out __2_____.
Patient Of course, whatever you need to do.
Doctor I will __3_____ an EKG and blood _____ to check if there is any damage in your heart.
Patient Wait, why do I need these tests?
Doctor These results __4_____ if you had any serious damage in the heart such as a heart attack.
Patient Oh, I see.
Doctor Also, we will give you a chest X-ray to rule out the possibility of a fracture __5_____ the pain.
Patient How long before we will get the results?
Doctor These tests don't __6_____, so if you wait here, I will come back with the results.
Patient OK, doctor. I'm worried now.
Doctor The pain can be caused __7_____, so let's just wait and see.
Patient Thank you. I hope it is nothing serious.
Doctor I will see you __8_____ then.
Patient I will wait here. Thank you.

Unit 7 Discussing Labs and Imaging   45

VOCABULARY

1 Please review the terms below. Draw lines to match each word to the correct definition.

1 How would patients describe their symptoms of pneumonia?

sweating • a. sputum that has visible streaks of blood

shivering • b. shaking throughout the body when the temperature drops below a level that the body finds comfortable

bloody mucus • c. the salty, colorless liquid which comes through the skin when a person is hot, ill, or afraid

2 How would patients describe their symptoms of asthma?

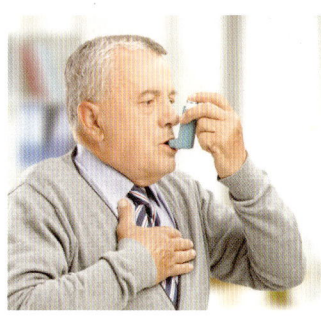

chest tightness • a. a high-pitched whistling sound that can occur when breathing and whilst having an attack

wheezing • b. an unpleasant sensation of heaviness or pressure in the chest

shortness of breath • c. an uncomfortable condition that makes it difficult to fully take air into the lungs

3 How would patients describe their symptoms of pleural effusion?

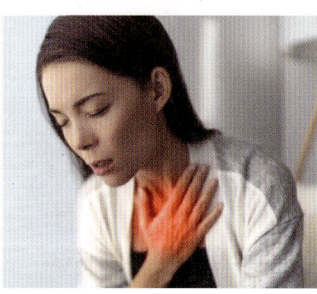

dry cough • a. a cough in which no phlegm or mucus is produced

difficulty breathing • b. spasms that occur when the diaphragm contracts continuously and involuntarily

persistent hiccups • c. an abnormal condition in which a person has a problem breathing normally when lying flat

2 Read the sentences below and complete them with words from **1**.

1 I'm coughing up _____ right now. I think there is something wrong with my lungs.

2 Can you hear a _____ when I breathe?

3 I have _____ and cannot stop them. It's so weird!

3 Match the structures with the definitions (A-H).

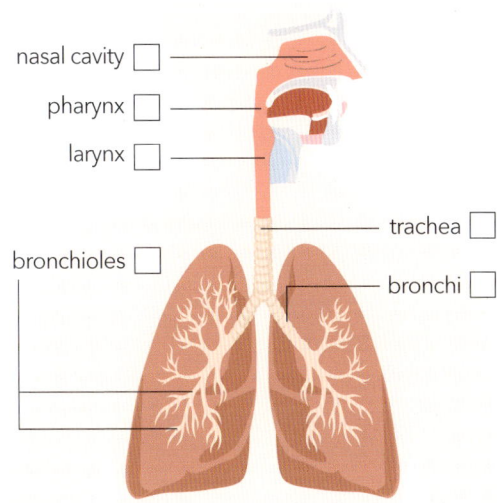

nasal cavity ☐
pharynx ☐
larynx ☐
trachea ☐
bronchioles ☐
bronchi ☐

A. a tube-shaped organ in the neck that contains the vocal cords
B. the membrane-lined cavity behind the nose and mouth, connecting them to the esophagus
C. a large, air-filled space above and behind the nose, located in the middle of the face
D. a tube-like section of the respiratory tract that connects the larynx with the bronchial parts of the lungs
E. the tiny branches of air tubes within the lungs that are a continuation of the bronchus
F. the large air passages that lead from the trachea (windpipe) to the lungs

REVIEW

Review the patient's complaint and complete the medical chart.

> I feel a shortness of breath and am worried that I may be having a heart attack. A history of heart attacks runs in my family. My father had one. I've been healthy for all my life without any disease.

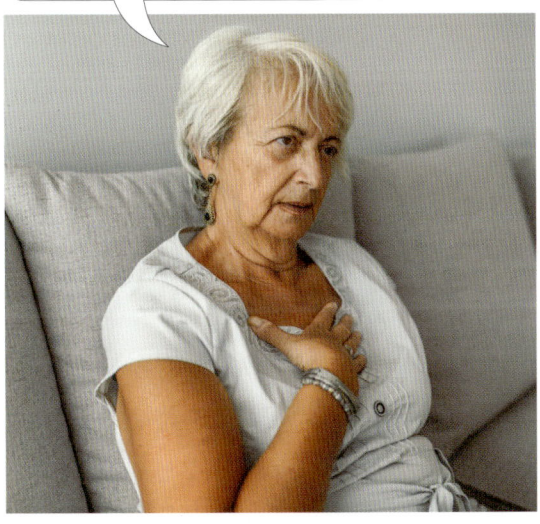

Patient Name:
Garcia THOMPSON, 54-yr-old, F

Chief complaint:
_____

Past medical history:
_____

Family history:
_____
_____
_____

Unit 7 Discussing Labs and Imaging   47

LISTENING

1 🎧 Listen to the conversation between a doctor and a patient.

2 Read the following statements and mark them as true (T) or false (F).

1 Mr. Daniels will need further tests. _____

2 The doctor is not concerned about Mr. Daniels's symptoms. _____

3 Mr. Daniels will need to come back tomorrow for another consultation. _____

4 Mr. Daniels might be able to go home today. _____

5 Mr. Daniels may need urgent treatment. _____

3 🎧 Listen again and choose the correct answers.

1 Which test is the doctor **NOT** ordering?
   a. chest X-ray
   b. basic blood test
   c. CT
   d. EKG

2 Which symptom does Mr. Daniels **NOT** currently have?
   a. shivering
   b. shortness of breath
   c. sweating
   d. chest tightness

3 Which systems does the doctor want to rule out issues with? (select all)
   a. cardiovascular
   b. digestive
   c. respiratory
   d. nervous

LANGUAGE POINT

1 Check how to use the expressions below and read the example sentences.

1 Let's see + if / how ...
e.g. Let's see if there are any abnormalities in your chest X-ray.
e.g. Let's see how you feel after taking the antibiotics.

2 We will see + if / how ...
e.g. We will see if there's an infection in the lungs.
e.g. We will see how you are able to follow the diet recommendations.

Note Both expressions are used to explain that a doctor wants to see the results of an action (e.g. taking meds, getting labs/imaging, or other treatments.)

2 Unscramble the words to complete the sentences.

1 Let's see _____.
(any urgent treatment / if you / the lab results / need / after / come back)

2 We will see _____.
(you / a follow-up appointment / if / need)

3 Let's see _____.
(how / help / the medications / you)

SPEAKING PRACTICE

1 With a partner, act out the roles below by using the expressions from Language Point. Then, switch roles.

Student A
You are the doctor. Discuss the topics below with Student B:
- recommended labs
- further imaging tests

Student B
You are the patient. Talk to Student A about your concerns regarding labs and imaging tests.

2 🎧 Below are some commonly mispronounced words. Listen carefully and repeat them out loud.

1 pharyngitis [far-in-**jahy**-tis]
2 bronchiolitis [brong-ke-o-**li**-tis]
3 pulse oximetry [puhls ok-**sim**-i-tree]
4 pleural effusion [**ploor**-uhl ih-**fyoo**-zhuhn]

Unit 7 Discussing Labs and Imaging   49

08
Discussing Test Results and the Diagnosis

Lesson objectives

After completing this lesson, you will be able to:
- Discuss test results with a patient.
- Discuss the diagnosis with a patient.

WARM UP

1 Please discuss the following questions:
- How is UTI diagnosed and treated?
- How is a kidney stone diagnosed and treated?

2 Match the correct word to each mnemonic and fill in the blanks.

Appendicitis
Biliary tract disease
Diverticulitis
Ovarian disease
Malignancy
Intestinal obstruction
Nephritic disorders
Acute pancreatitis
Liquor (ethanol)

Mnemonics for abdominal pain, acute, differential diagnosis: "ABDOMINAL"

A _____
B _____
D _____
O _____
M _____
I _____
N _____
A _____
L _____

3 Here are some possible causes of a patient's abdominal pain. Match each word with the corresponding definition.

Appendicitis •   a. a blockage that keeps food or liquid from passing through small or large intestines

Biliary tract disease •   b. the infection or inflammation of pouches that can form in the intestines.

Diverticulitis •   c. kidney disease involving inflammation

Ovarian disease •   d. conditions that occur in young women and can affect their reproductive systems and general health

Malignancy •   e. a serious medical condition in which the appendix becomes inflamed and causes pain

Intestinal obstruction •   f. sudden inflammation of the pancreas

Nephritic disorders •   g. disease affecting the bile ducts, gallbladder and other structures involved in the production and transportation of bile

Acute pancreatitis •   h. a strong alcoholic drink

Liquor (ethanol) •   i. the state or presence of a tumor; cancer

EXPRESSIONS

1 You have a 44-year-old male patient with symptoms of a stroke. Read the questions/statements given by the doctor and match them with the appropriate response.

Doctor says...
1. OK, Mr. Delacruz. It's good that you came to the hospital immediately.   **d**
2. We got your CT scan results back.   **a**
3. Well, can you see the blockage here on the film?   **b**
4. One of your blood vessels here is blocked with clots.   **c**
5. Yes, all of your symptoms are related to a stroke.   **g**
6. It's called an ischemic stroke.   **h**
7. I will give you an injection to break up the clots.   **e**
8. We will need to see the results of the injections before we can tell what further treatments might be needed.   **f**

Patient says...
a. OK. What do you see?
b. Yes. I can see it.
c. Oh, is that causing my dizziness?
d. Yes, I came here as soon as I could.
e. Is that all the treatment I will need?
f. OK. Thank you, doctor.
g. So, what exactly is my diagnosis?
h. What is the treatment for that?

2 Complete the dialogue below with the expressions from the box.

- to take at home
- I suspected
- basically
- the full course of
- there is evidence of
- the results are negative
- arrived

Doctor Hi, Mr. Ryals, your test results have __1 arrived__.
Patient OK, doctor. Is there something wrong with the results?
Doctor Well, __2 I suspected__ a urinary tract infection since you have cloudy urine and a constant urge to urinate.
Patient Yes, you mentioned earlier that might be a possibility.
Doctor Your urinalysis does indeed show that __3 there is evidence of__ an infection.
Patient Can you explain that further? How do you know there is an infection?
Doctor Well __4 basically__, we found bacteria and white blood cells in your urine sample.
Patient Ah, OK, I understand.
Doctor Also we did a test for sexually transmitted diseases and __5 the results are negative__, which is very good.
Patient Oh, that is good to hear.
Doctor As it's your first time to have these symptoms, I will prescribe antibiotics __6 to take at home__.
Patient OK, thank you.
Doctor You must take __7 the full course of__ antibiotics to ensure that your infection is cured.
Patient I will take them all. No worries, doctor.

VOCABULARY

1 Please review the terms below. Draw lines to match each word to the correct definition.

1 How would patients describe their symptoms of a UTI?

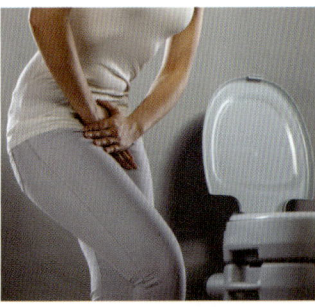

urge to urinate • a. not transparent or clear liquid

burning feeling • b. pain or discomfort during urination

cloudy urine • c. the sudden, urgent need to pee; can be accompanied by bladder leaks before making it to the restroom

2 How would patients describe their symptoms of a kidney stone?

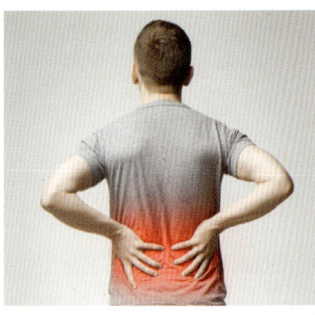

flank pain • a. having an extremely unpleasant smell while urinating

foul-smelling urine • b. discomfort in the upper abdomen, back, and/or sides

vomiting • c. the act of emptying the contents of the stomach through the mouth

3 How would patients describe their symptoms of kidney failure?

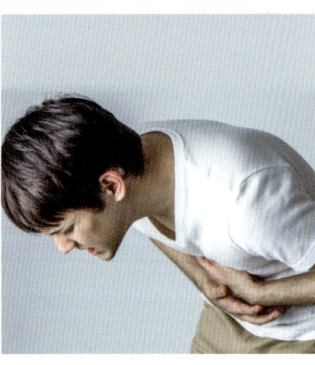

fluid retention • a. excess fluids that build up inside the body

seizure • b. producing less urine than normal

urinating less frequently • c. a sudden, uncontrollable electrical disturbance in the brain; it can cause changes in behavior, movements, or feelings, as well as in levels of consciousness

2 Read the sentences below and complete them with the words from **1**. Change the word form if necessary.

1 I cannot hold my pee. I have had this _____ all morning.

2 I've been _____ since last night.

3 I felt like _____ and nauseous last night. I don't know what's wrong with me.

3 Match the structures with the definitions (A-D).

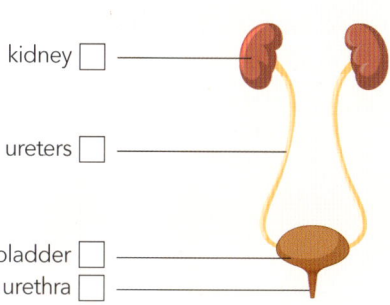

kidney ☐
ureters ☐
bladder ☐
urethra ☐

A. a round, bag-like organ that stores urine and is located in the pelvic area which is just below the kidneys and right behind the pelvic bone
B. tubes that carry urine from the kidney to the bladder
C. two bean-shaped organs in the renal system which help the body pass waste as urine; filters blood before sending it back to the heart
D. a tube that carries urine from the bladder to outside of the body

REVIEW

Review the patient's complaint and complete the medical chart.

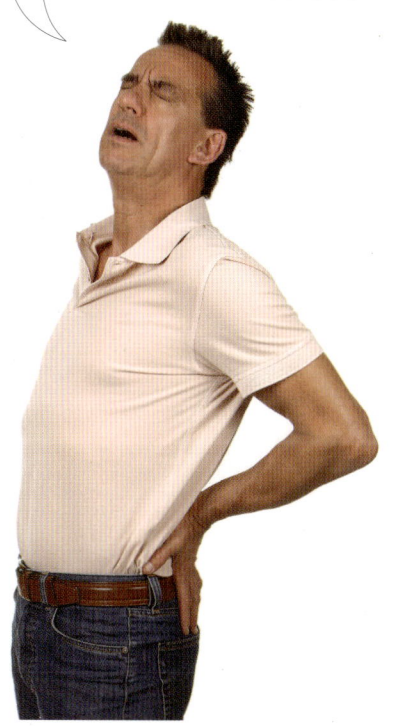

I have had terrible back pain since this morning. I've had urinary tract infections and kidney stones many times in the past.

Patient Name:
Eric SCHELLER, 52-yr-old, M

Chief complaint:
_____
_____
_____

Past medical history:
_____
_____
_____
_____

LISTENING

1 🎧 Listen to the conversation between a doctor and a patient.

2 Read the following statements and mark them as true (T) or false (F).

1. Mr. White is diagnosed with appendicitis. _____
2. The doctor is explaining the test results to Mr. White. _____
3. There is an abnormality in Mr. White's intestinal organs. _____
4. Mr. White doesn't know his diagnosis. _____
5. Mr. White will need to be admitted. _____

3 🎧 Listen again and choose the correct answers.

1. Which test result confirmed Mr. White's diagnosis?
    a. X-ray
    b. ultrasound
    c. CT
    d. urine test

2. According to the conversation, which symptom does Mr. Daniels currently have?
    a. urge to urinate
    b. flank pain
    c. fluid retention
    d. vomiting

3. What is Mr. White's diagnosis?
    a. urinary tract infection
    b. appendicitis
    c. renal failure
    d. kidney stones

LANGUAGE POINT

1 Check how to use the expressions below and read the example sentences.

1 You need to + *Infinitive Verb*.
: used to inform a patient of what actions to do or what instructions to follow
- e.g. You need to stop smoking and also stop drinking alcohol.
- e.g. You need to take your blood pressure every day before taking the medication.

2 You will need to + *Infinitive Verb* + *if-clause*
: used to inform a patient what actions to do or what instructions to follow in the possible future
- e.g. You will need to call 911 if you feel any more chest pain.
- e.g. You will need to get a CT if your back pain doesn't improve.

Note Both expressions are used to inform a patient of what should be done. However, by using different tenses, expression #1 talks about actions that should be done in a patient's daily routine while #2 talks about actions that should be done if a certain situation occurs in the future.

2 Fill in the blanks using the correct form of the verbs in the brackets.
1. You (need / will need) to take this medication every morning starting today.
2. You (need / will need) to take this medication if you develop a migraine.
3. You (need / will need) to take the full course of antibiotics immediately.

SPEAKING PRACTICE

1 With a partner, act out the roles below by using the expressions from Language Point. Then, switch roles.

Student A
You are the doctor. Discuss the topics below with Student B:
- test results
- differential diagnosis

Student B
You are the patient. Talk to Student A about your concerns regarding test results and diagnosis.

2 Below are some commonly mispronounced words. Listen carefully and repeat them out loud.
1. cystitis [si-**stahy**-tis]
2. pyelonephritis [pahy-uh-loh-nuh-**frahy**-tis] [pahy-el-oh-nuh-**frahy**-tis]
3. urethritis [yoo r-uh-**thrahy**-tis]
4. lithotripsy [**lith**-uh-trip-see]

09
Developing Empathic Communication Skills

Lesson Objectives

After completing this lesson, you will be able to:
- Better recognize patients' emotions.
- Empathize with patients.

WARM UP

1 Please discuss the following questions:
- How do you help a patient who doesn't want to be helped?
- How do you convince a patient to see a psychiatrist?

2 Match the correct word to each mnemonic and fill in the blanks.

Affect flat

Weight change (loss or gain)

Energy, loss of

Sad feelings / Suicidal thoughts

Others (guilt, loss of pleasure, hopeless)

Memory loss

Emotional blunting

Mnemonics for signs and symptoms of depression: "AWESOME"

A _____
W _____
E _____
S _____
O _____
M _____
E _____

3 Here are some words that are related to signs and symptoms of depression. Match each word with the corresponding definition.

Affect flat •

Weight change (loss or gain) •

Energy, loss of •

Sad feelings / Suicidal thoughts •

Others (guilt, loss of pleasure, hopeless) •

Memory loss •

Emotional blunting •

a. described as tiredness, weariness, lethargy, or fatigue

b. lack of interest in or pleasure from activities that were once enjoyed

c. a reduction in or a lack of emotional expression

d. thinking about, considering, or planning suicide

e. dulled feelings and emotions

f. a change in body weight resulting from either voluntary (diet, exercise) or involuntary (illness) circumstances

g. the forgetting of information and experiences that a person would normally be able to recall easily

EXPRESSIONS

1 You have a 46-year-old female patient with symptoms of depression. Read the questions/statements given by the doctor and match them with the appropriate response.

Doctor says...
1. Will you tell me more about your depression? __c__
2. I'm so sorry you feel that way. _____
3. Have you tried to talk about your emotions with someone else? _____
4. Was it helpful for you? _____
5. It's always good to seek professional help if you are experiencing depression. _____
6. Also, I'm here to help. So please feel free to talk to me about anything. _____
7. Sure, that's fine. Take your time. _____

Patient says...
a. I see. Thanks for your advice.
b. A little bit but not much.
c. I'm here because I just feel hopeless.
d. Yes, I've discussed it with my husband before.
e. I just don't know why I'm so sad all the time.
f. OK, doctor. If it is okay with you, let me start from the beginning.
g. My depression started about a year ago.

2 Complete the dialogue below with the expressions from the box.

- Again, I'm so sorry for
- sorry to hear
- Please do
- discuss anything with
- as soon as possible
- but unfortunately
- please feel free

Doctor I am so __1_____ about the loss of your father.
Patient I cannot believe it. He was always so strong and healthy.
Doctor Your father had emergency surgery, __2_____ the surgeon couldn't stop the bleeding.
Patient I don't know what to do now without him.
Doctor You can __3_____ our team. We are here to help.
Patient That's so kind of you.
Doctor We also have a chaplain here in the hospital if this would help you.
Patient Oh really? Can I meet him?
Doctor Yes of course. __4_____. I can arrange a meeting __5_____ if you would like.
Patient That would be great.
Doctor Also, if you want to talk to me or our team, __6_____ to contact us anytime.
Patient Thank you for your offer.
Doctor __7_____ your loss.
Patient Thank you, doctor.

Unit 9 Developing Empathic Communication Skills

VOCABULARY

1 Please review the terms below. Draw lines to match each word to the correct definition.

1 How would patients describe their psychological symptoms of depression?

bad mood • a. having no expectation of good results or of success

hopeless • b. thinking about, considering, or planning to end one's own life

suicidal thoughts • c. an angry or irritable state of mind

2 How would patients describe their physical symptoms of depression?

constipation • a. changes in the desire to eat

difficulty falling / staying asleep • b. being unable to empty the bowels as often as they should be emptied

changes in appetite • c. regularly occurring issues with sleep; finding it hard to fall asleep and/or waking up several times during the night

3 How would you recognize suicidal behavior?

sudden calmness • a. becoming calm after a period of depression or moodiness; a sign that the person has made a decision to end his or her life

withdrawal • b. engaging in potentially dangerous activities such as reckless driving, unsafe sex, increased use of drugs and/or alcohol; a behavior that might indicate that the person no longer values his or her life

self-harmful behavior • c. choosing to be alone and avoiding friends or social activities

2 Read the sentences below and complete them with words from **1**.

1 Sorry doctor, but I feel _____. I can't see any future in my life.

2 I have had _____ recently. I wake up every 1 or 2 hours during the night.

3 Ms. Waibel, I'm worried about your _____. When did you first start harming yourself?

3 Match the stages with the definitions (A-E).

denial ☐ anger ☐ bargaining ☐ depression ☐ acceptance ☐

A. the stage in which the patient tries to delay the end by bargaining in an attempt to avoid the unavoidable
B. the stage in which most people can't continue denying impending death or the loss of a loved one and denial soon gives way to feelings of anger, rage, jealousy, and hatred
C. the stage in which the patient and their family do not believe the announcement of impending death and often believe that a mistake has been made in the diagnosis
D. the stage that focuses on a deep sense of loss and is felt in varying degrees from person to person
E. the final stage that is about accepting the new reality

REVIEW

Read the patient's complaint and complete the medical chart.

> I'm afraid I may do something terrible to myself like my mother did to herself. I smoke a ton of cigarettes every day and I can't sleep without alcohol.
> I don't know what to do.

Patient Name:
Grace GELLER, 62-yr-old, F

Chief complaint:
_____

Past medical history: anxiety, depression

Family history: Mother died by suicide at age 67.

Social history:
_____

Review of systems: constipation, sleep problems,

LISTENING

1 🎧 Listen to the conversation between a doctor and a patient.

2 Read the following statements and mark the following as true (T) or false (F).

1 Ms. Ann is willing to talk to the doctor about her concerns. _____

2 The doctor is trying to convince Ms. Ann to talk about her condition. _____

3 Ms. Ann is living with her husband at home. _____

4 Ms. Ann shared her emotions with her friend. _____

5 Ms. Ann will seek professional help. _____

3 🎧 Listen again and choose the correct answers.

1 Which symptom does Ms. Ann **NOT** talk about?

   a. hopelessness
   b. changes in appetite
   c. loss of energy
   d. difficulty falling / staying asleep

2 What symptom is Ms. Ann most worried about?

   a. bad mood
   b. suicidal thoughts
   c. weight change
   d. constipation

3 What is Ms. Ann's next plan?

   a. to see a psychiatrist
   b. to see the same doctor
   c. no further plan
   d. to see a psychologist

LANGUAGE POINT

1 Check how to use the expressions below and read the example sentences.

1 Would you + *Infinitive Verb*?

: used to ask a question or request something of someone

e.g. Would you please describe your situation to me?

e.g. Would you tell me a little more about the kinds of problems you're having?

2 I would + *Infinitive Verb*.

: used to politely express opinions/suggestions

e.g. I would suggest that you admit yourself to undergo observation for a couple of days.

e.g. If possible, I would encourage you to talk about your feelings.

2 Make a complete sentence by unscrambling the words below.

1 _____?
(to see me / for a follow-up / Would you come / in two days)

2 _____.
(we talk again / I would suggest / if you have / that / any more concerns)

3 _____?
(for treatments / Would you agree / a psychiatrist / to see)

SPEAKING PRACTICE

1 With a partner, act out the roles below by using the expressions from Language Point. Then, switch roles.

Student A

You are the doctor. Discuss the topics below with Student B:
- coping with depression and suicidal thoughts
- seeking professional help and treatment

Student B

You are the patient. Talk to Student A about your concerns regarding depression and suicidal thoughts.

2 Below are some commonly mispronounced words. Listen carefully and repeat them out loud.

1 suicide [**soo**-uh-sahyd]
2 anxiety [ang-**zahy**-i-tee]
3 insomnia [in-**som**-nee-uh]
4 anorexia [an-uh-**rek**-see-uh]

10 Describing Treatment Options

Lesson Objectives

After completing this lesson, you will be able to:
- Discuss treatment options with patients.

WARM UP

1 Please discuss the following questions:
- How does trauma affect physical health?
- What are the most common types of trauma? (e.g. a road accident)

2 Match the correct word to each mnemonic and fill in the blanks.

| Deformities & Discolorations | Contusions | Swelling & Symmetry | Tenderness |
| Abrasions & Avulsion | Burns | Penetrations & Punctures | Lacerations |

Mnemonics for trauma assessment: "DCAP-BTLS"

D _____   B _____
C _____   T _____
A _____   L _____
P _____   S _____

3 Here are some words used regarding trauma assessment. Draw lines to match each term with the corresponding definition.

Deformities & Discolorations •
Contusions •
Abrasions & Avulsion •
Penetrations & Punctures •
Burns •
Tenderness •
Lacerations •
Swelling & Symmetry •

a. the surface layers of the skin (epidermis) are broken; a medical term for a ripping or tearing of the skin or body part

b. an injury caused by exposure to heat or flame

c. pain or discomfort when an affected area is touched

d. an abnormal enlargement of a body part, typically as a result of an accumulation of fluid

e. a major abnormality in the shape of a body part or organ compared to the normal shape of that part; a change in something's color, usually for the worse

f. an object going through the body with force; a small hole in something such as the skin, caused by a sharp object

g. injuries to bones, muscles, and the tissue just under the skin that can cause bruises; a medical term for a bruise.

h. deep cuts or a wound that is produced by the tearing of soft body tissue

EXPRESSIONS

1 You have a 55-year-old male patient with post-traumatic stress disorder (PTSD). Read the statements given by the doctor and match them with the appropriate response.

Doctor says...
1. I would like to discuss possible treatment options with you.   __f__
2. My first recommendation would be to treat you with cognitive behavior therapy.   _____
3. It is a type of psychotherapy and it is known to be one of the most effective treatments for PTSD.   _____
4. Well, I also recommend that you start anti-anxiety medication. It will help relieve severe anxiety and other related issues.   _____
5. I'm sorry, but PTSD is not strictly curable. However, the combination of therapy and medication can make a big difference.   _____
6. Sounds good. I will write you a referral letter in case you want to make an appointment.   _____

Patient says...
a. If I take the medication, will my PTSD be cured?
b. Thank you very much doctor.
c. I will discuss this with my wife and let you know my decision.
d. I see. What other options are there?
e. What kind of therapy is that?
f. OK. What options do I have?

2 Complete the dialogue below with the expressions from the box.

• who can oversee	• teach ... about	• there are ... available	• suggest ... consult
• questions or concerns	• I recommend	• it will help ... with	• perform daily activities

Doctor Now we will need to discuss additional treatment options for after your discharge.

Patient Yes. I remember you told me that rehabilitation will be required because of my brain injury.

Doctor That's right. Actually, **1**_____ various rehabilitation specialists _____.

Patient Which ones do I need?

Doctor First, **2**_____ that you keep seeing a psychiatrist **3**_____ the whole rehabilitation process.

Patient Sure. That seems like a good plan.

Doctor You will also need to see a physical therapist for a while because **4**_____ you _____ your mobility, walking, and balance.

Patient During my stay in the hospital, physical therapy helped me a lot.

Doctor I also **5**_____ that you _____ with a speech pathologist who can help you improve your communication skills.

Patient Yeah, I definitely think I will need that as I'm having some difficulties with my speech.

Doctor And lastly, there is a traumatic brain injury specialist who can help coordinate your care and **6**_____ your family _____ the trauma and recovery process.

Patient That would be great.

Doctor The goal is to improve your ability to **7**_____.

Patient I understand. It all sounds reasonable.

Doctor Do you have any **8**_____ so far?

Patient No, doctor. I think I'm good.

Unit 10 Describing Treatment Options   63

VOCABULARY

1 Please review the terms below. Draw lines to match each word with the correct definition.

1 What kinds of physical trauma symptoms can a patient experience?

lethargy • a. sudden, intense surge of fear, panic, and/or anxiety

paleness • b. a feeling of sleepiness, fatigue, or sluggishness

panic attack • c. unnatural lack of color in the skin

2 What kinds of symptoms can a patient experience when they have a fracture?

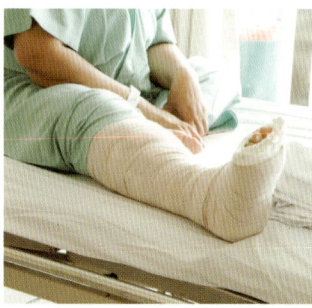

inability to bear weight • a. a patient can't put any weight on an injured body part (generally referring to a fractured leg, ankle, or foot)

loss of function • b. symptom that usually occurs immediately after the fracture

acute pain • c. not being able to move body parts properly due to the disturbed structure of a patient's bones

3 What kinds of symptoms can a patient have when experiencing post-traumatic stress disorder (PTSD)?

flashback • a. a disturbing dream that wakes one up, generally associated with negative feelings such as anxiety or fear

nightmare • b. a feeling that the trauma is happening again

feeling of isolation • c. a feeling of sadness or distress about being alone or feeling disconnected from the surrounding world

2 Read the sentences below and complete them with the words from **1**.

1 I'm having a _____ right now. I can't breathe and I am freaking out.

2 I'm having _____ in my hips. It started right after I fell.

3 Doctor, I have a hard time falling back to sleep after I have a _____.

3 Match the structures with the definitions (A-E).

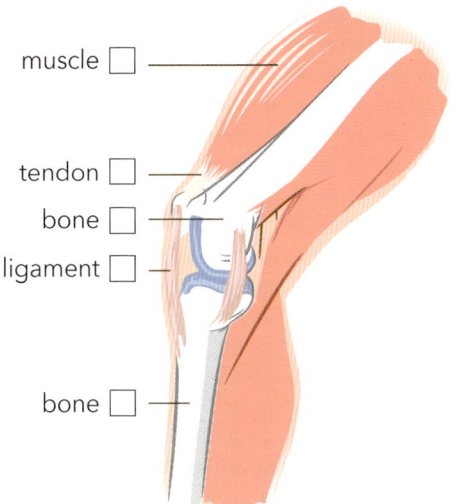

muscle ☐
tendon ☐
bone ☐
ligament ☐
bone ☐

A. a tissue composed of cells or fibers, the contraction of which produces movement in the body

B. structure that provides a rigid framework as well as support for other parts of the body; it plays an important role in the movement of the body and protects many of the internal organs

C. a fibrous connective tissue which attaches muscle to bones and serves to move the bones

D. a fibrous connective tissue that connects bones to other bones and gives the joints support while also limiting their movement

REVIEW

Review the patient's complaint and complete the medical chart.

"I was in a traffic accident. I was alert right after it happened, but then quickly started to develop a headache. I have never had any medical problems before this."

**Patient Name:
Kimberly YOUNG, 62-yr-old, F**

Chief complaint:
_____

Past medical history:
_____
_____

Family history: no FH

Social history: never smoked, currently participates in sports

Review of systems: no loss of consciousness, alert, eye movements are normal, voice is normal, right forehead, upper lip, and nasal lacerations. Equal muscle strength

Unit 10 Describing Treatment Options

LISTENING

1 🎧 Listen to the conversation between a doctor and a patient.

2 Read the following statements and mark them as true (T) or false (F).

1 The doctor is discussing treatment options with the patient right now. _____
2 The patient is 90 years old. _____
3 The patient will need physical therapy after surgery. _____
4 The surgery will take place today. _____
5 The patient is on antibiotics due to pneumonia. _____

3 🎧 Listen again and choose the correct answers.

1 What other illnesses does the patient **NOT** have?
   a. dementia
   b. diabetes
   c. pneumonia
   d. hypertension

2 Which complication does the doctor **NOT** mention?
   a. blood clots
   b. infection
   c. stroke
   d. panic attack

3 Which symptom does the doctor **NOT** mention if the fracture is to be left without surgery?
   a. swelling
   b. tenderness
   c. infection
   d. worsening pain

LANGUAGE POINT

1 Check how to use the expressions below and read the example sentences.

1 It is necessary to + *Infinitive Verb*.

: used to give a patient a strong recommendation or suggestion

e.g. It is necessary to have surgery right away. We can't delay it any longer.

e.g. It is necessary to take medication if you feel a panic attack coming on.

2 It is hard to + *Infinitive Verb*.

: used to express opinions about actions that are difficult to do

e.g. It is hard to predict a discharge date right now. We need to monitor your improvement first.

e.g. It is hard to make a diagnosis without a confirmed result from the CT imaging.

Note "It is + Adjective + to + Infinitive Verb" expression is used to talk about facts or opinions. Please make sure that you use an infinitive verb when using the expression.

2 Circle the most appropriate word for each sentence.

1. It is (necessary / unnecessary) to be admitted today. That way she will get better sooner.
2. It is (hard / easy) to find the exact cause of your dizziness but we should rule out the possibility of a stroke first.
3. It is (necessary / unnecessary) to call 911 immediately if you are having any chest pain.

SPEAKING PRACTICE

1 With a partner, act out the roles below by using the expressions from Language Point. Then, switch roles.

Student A

You are the doctor. Discuss the topics below with Student B:
- surgical treatment options for a traumatic injury
- conservative treatment options for fractures

Student B

You are the patient. Talk to Student A about your concerns regarding treatment options.

2 Below are some commonly mispronounced words. Listen carefully and repeat them out loud.

1. conscious [**kon**-shuhs]
2. amputation [**am**-pyoo-**tey**-shuhn]
3. resuscitation [ri-suhs-i-**tey**-shuhn]
4. ligament [**lig**-uh-muhnt]

11 Educating Patients on Lifestyle Changes

Lesson Objectives

After completing this lesson, you will be able to:
- Educate patients on lifestyle modifications.
- Discuss the benefits of lifestyle modifications.

WARM UP

1 Please discuss the following questions:
- How can obesity be prevented?
- Who is most at risk for obesity? (ex. low-income)

2 Match the correct word to each mnemonic and fill in the blanks.

Weight control
Alcohol reduction
Smoking cessation
Health promotion
Exercise
Diet

Mnemonics for lifestyle modification in obesity: "WASHED"

W _____
A _____
S _____
H _____
E _____
D _____

3 How would you educate your patient who is obese and needs a lifestyle modification? Match each term to the appropriate statement.

Weight control •

Alcohol reduction •

Smoking cessation •

Health promotion •

Exercise •

Diet •

a. Losing weight can mean a reduction of risk for heart disease, diabetes, and cancer.

b. Quitting significantly reduces the risk of dying from diseases such as lung cancer, coronary heart disease, and chronic obstructive pulmonary disease.

c. It involves a process in which one develops a healthier lifestyle to help prevent illness and disabilities.

d. By limiting consumption of, or cutting out alcohol, the caloric intake will decrease as long as the alcohol is not replaced with another high-calorie substitute.

e. It is a plan that involves eating whole-grain foods, fruit, vegetables, and fat-free or low-dairy products while reducing the consumption of foods with trans fats, cholesterol, sugars, and salt.

f. Doing activities that put the least amount of stress on the joints like walking, swimming, or water aerobics.

EXPRESSIONS

1 You are educating a mother who has an obese 10-year-old son. Read the questions/statements given by the doctor and match them with the appropriate response.

Doctor says...
1. Did you know that the obesity rate for children aged 6 to 11 has more than quadrupled during the past 40 years? ____d____
2. Yes, and there are so many other issues with childhood obesity. Children with obesity are often bullied more than their normal-weight peers. _____
3. Obese children are also more likely to experience depression and low self-esteem. _____
4. Children with obesity are also at higher risk for having other chronic illnesses such as diabetes, asthma, joint problems, sleep apnea, and heart disease. _____
5. And children with obesity are more likely to continue to struggle with obesity as adults. _____
6. You should consider helping your son to make a lifestyle change. _____

Mother says...
a. My boy has been having some problems at school.
b. I can see that. He does seem unhappy from time to time.
c. I really don't want my boy to grow up being overweight.
d. Really? No, I have never heard that before.
e. What can I do?
f. Oh no, I didn't know that!

2 Complete the dialogue below with the expressions from the box.

• stay active	• good to limit	• you can do	• easy to adjust
• healthy eating habits	• sedentary time	• give ... plenty of	• no more than

Doctor So let's talk about some lifestyle modifications _1_____ at home.
Patient Yes, please continue.
Doctor Your son needs to develop _2_____.
Patient He is a picky eater and only ever wants fast food.
Doctor You still need to _3_____ him _____ vegetables, fruits, and whole-grain foods.
Patient OK. I will try my best.
Doctor It's _4_____ sugary beverages.
Patient I will not buy them anymore.
Doctor You should help your son _5_____. He should do at least 60 minutes of physical activity everyday.
Patient He hates moving. He spends all his time playing video games.
Doctor You really need to help your son avoid too much _6_____. Try to monitor how much time he spends watching television or playing video games.
Patient Well, I will try. How long is it okay for him to be playing his game?
Doctor I'd say _7_____ 2 hours a day.
Patient That will be challenging but I will try.
Doctor It may not be _8_____ to in the beginning but you should give it your best try.
Patient Thank you for the advice.

VOCABULARY

1 Please review the terms below. Draw lines to match each word to the correct definition.

1 What types of symptoms will patients present with when they are obese?

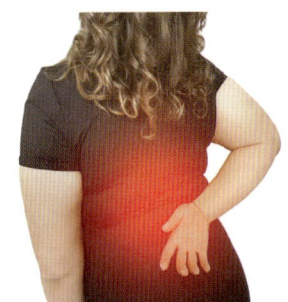

joint pain • a. diseases or disorders that affect the skin

backache • b. pains arising from any part of a joint including cartilage, bone, ligaments, tendons, or muscles

skin problems • c. a pain, especially in the lumbar region of the back, usually caused by the strain of a muscle or ligament

2 What types of symptoms will patients present with when they are obese?

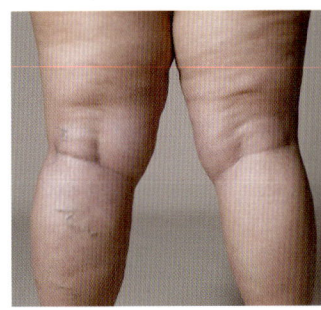

heartburn • a. the time between menstruation starts to change; the number of days that the period lasts varies a great deal; losing more or less blood during a period than usual

irregular periods •

b. enlarged, swollen, and twisting veins

varicose veins • c. a painful burning feeling in one's chest or throat

3 What types of symptoms will patients present with when they are obese?

snoring • a. noisy breathing during sleep

low self-esteem • b. sweating more than might be expected based on the surrounding temperature, activity level, or stress

increased sweating • c. a lack of confidence and feeling badly about oneself

2 Read the sentences below and complete them with words from **1**.

1 I have _____. My knees and shoulders hurt badly.

2 Look at my calf. I have _____.

3 I know that I have _____. I hate looking at myself in a mirror.

3 Match the terms with the definitions (A-E).

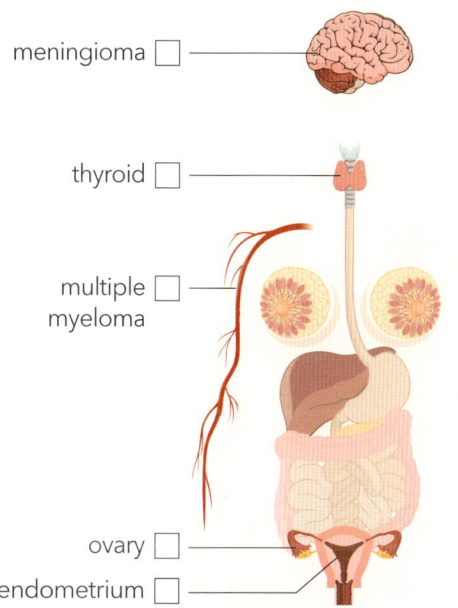

meningioma ☐
thyroid ☐
multiple myeloma ☐
ovary ☐
endometrium ☐

A. a cancer that forms in a type of white blood cell called a plasma cell
B. a butterfly-shaped gland that is located at the front of the neck, below the Adam's apple, and makes a hormone that controls how fast the heart beats and how fast calories are burned
C. the layer in which the implantation (the stage of pregnancy) takes place
D. brain tumors that develop from the membrane (the "meninges") that covers the brain and spinal cord
E. the organ that produces and releases eggs (oocytes) into the female reproductive tract at the mid-point of each menstrual cycle

REVIEW

Review the patient's complaint and complete the medical chart.

"I have irregular periods, heartburn, and joint pain. Both of my parents have hypertension and diabetes. I smoke cigarettes and drink alcohol daily."

Patient Name:
Kearney BROWN, 32-yr-old, F

Chief complaint: _____

Past medical history: hypothyroidism

Family history: _____

Social history: _____

Review of systems: isolation from colleagues, lack of social relationships, anxiety, depression, binge-eating disorder

LISTENING

1 🎧 Listen to the conversation between a doctor and a patient.

2 Read the following statements and mark the following as true (T) or false (F).

1. Mr. Higdon's current symptoms are related to his excess weight gain. _____
2. Mr. Higdon is obese and has hypertension. _____
3. The doctor provides some examples of exercise. _____
4. Mr. Higdon is not willing to change his lifestyle. _____
5. The doctor provides some information regarding diet modification. _____

3 🎧 Listen again and choose the correct answers.

1. Mr. Higdon is experiencing several symptoms except which one?
   a. joint pains
   b. varicose veins
   c. heartburn
   d. increased sweating

2. Which medical condition does the doctor mention could occur if Mr. Higdon's diabetes continues to be unmonitored?
   a. stroke
   b. heart attack
   c. dry, itchy skin
   d. vision problems

3. Which medical condition does the doctor mention the client is at high risk for because of his obesity?
   a. joint problems
   b. gallbladder disease
   c. thyroid disease
   d. psychological problems

LANGUAGE POINT

1 Check how to use the expressions below and read the example sentences.

1 You should (not) + *Infinitive Verb*.

: used to give suggestions or advice on a patient's lifestyle

e.g. You should do activities like walking, swimming, or water aerobics. These will put the least amount of stress on your joints.

e.g. You should not consume any foods that are high in fat, cholesterol, sugar, or salt.

2 You must (not) + *Infinitive Verb*.

: used when wanting to give strongly worded suggestions or advice

e.g. You must quit smoking. Otherwise, you are more at risk of having a heart attack.

e.g. You must not drive your vehicle after taking this medication as you can experience drowsiness.

Note "You should not ~" is used to talk about things that are not recommended for patients to do. "You must not~" is used to give stronger advice to patients. It is used to talk about things that will cause problems.

2 Circle the most appropriate word for each sentence.

1. You (should / should not) try to eat balanced meals including whole-grain foods, daily fruit, and vegetables.
2. You (should / should not) develop healthy eating habits to prevent illness.
3. You (must / must not) drink any alcohol until you are off the medication.

SPEAKING PRACTICE

1 With a partner, act out the roles below by using the expressions from Language Point. Then, switch roles.

Student A

You are the doctor. Talk with Student B about:
- the benefits of lifestyle modifications
- how to achieve a successful lifestyle

Student B

You are the patient. Talk to Student A about the obstacles you will face when changing your lifestyle.

2 Below are some commonly mispronounced words. Listen carefully and repeat them out loud.

1. obesity [oh-**bee**-si-tee]
2. endometrium [en-doh-**mee**-tree-uhm]
3. thyroid [**thahy**-roid]
4. varicose veins [**var**-i-kohs veyns]

12
Discussing Referrals and Admission

Lesson Objectives

After completing this lesson, you will be able to:
- Discuss referrals with patients.
- Discuss admission arrangements with patients.

WARM UP

1 Please discuss the following questions:
- What are the early warning signs of sepsis?
- How do doctors test for Meniere's disease?

2 Match the correct word to each mnemonic and fill in the blanks.

- Extreme pain or general discomfort ("worst ever")
- Shivering, fever, or very cold
- Pale or discolored skin
- Sleepy, difficult to rouse, confused
- "I feel like I might die"
- Short of breath

Mnemonics for symptoms of sepsis: "SEPSIS"

S _____
E _____
P _____
S _____
I _____
S _____

3 Here are the most common sources of SEPSIS. Draw lines to match each word with the corresponding definition.

- Meningitis
- Skin or soft tissue infection
- Pneumonia
- Catheter-related infection
- Peritonitis
- Urinary tract infection
- Infection of unknown source

a. infection(s) in one or both lungs caused by bacteria, viruses, and fungi.

b. infection(s) in any part of the urinary system — the kidneys, ureters, bladder, and/or urethra

c. infection(s) which can be caused by a variety of bacteria or other microorganisms that enter the skin through wounds, burns, and/or irritated skin

d. presence of bacteremia originating from an intravenous catheter

e. no explanation for an elevated temperature, despite investigation by a physician

f. an acute inflammation of the protective membranes covering the brain and spinal cord

g. a serious condition in which the covering of the stomach, intestines, and nearby organs become swollen and infected.

EXPRESSIONS

1 You have a 65-year-old male patient with suspected Meniere's disease. Read the statements given by the doctor and match them with the appropriate response.

Doctor says...
1. Mr. Bacal, your current symptoms are related to Meniere's disease. However, we need to rule out other possibilities.   **d**
2. You will need to consult with a neurologist to find out if the dizziness is caused by neurologic reasons.   ____
3. A tumor in the brain or multiple sclerosis can cause problems similar to those of Meniere's disease.   ____
4. No, Mr. Bacal. It's just precautionary.   ____
5. Yes, we should rule out these possibilities quickly. I'm writing a referral letter so you can schedule an appointment as soon as possible.   ____
6. If that is the case, then I will prescribe some medications that will help. And you will need to come back again for a follow-up.   ____
7. Please contact us right away if you notice any changes in your symptoms.   ____

Patient says...
a. So then, is it necessary that I go see a neurologist right away?
b. What kind of neurologic reasons are we talking about?
c. Oh, I see. I will contact the doctor today then. What happens if the checkup turns out to be normal?
d. OK. What do we need to do to figure it out?
e. OK. I will call you if I notice anything.
f. Do I need to be worried?
g. Thank you very much, doctor. I hope it is nothing serious.

2 Complete the dialogue below with the expressions from the box.

• under close observation	• responding to	• refer … to	• receive … intravenously
• spread through	• arrange an admission		• take good care of

Doctor Ms. Francis, your leg infection is not **1**_____ the oral antibiotic that you have been taking.

Patient Yes, you are right. It's not getting any better. I can feel it getting warmer and you can see that it is more swollen than before.

Doctor Your symptoms are getting more severe and your fever is spiking. I would like to **2**_____ you _____ an infectious disease specialist.

Patient Why do I need to see a specialist?

Doctor You may need to be hospitalized and **3**_____ antibiotics _____. It can be serious if not treated promptly. We don't want any infections to **4**_____ the body.

Patient Oh, I see. How long will I need to stay in the hospital?

Doctor You may need to stay for 3 to 5 days **5**_____ and receive daily wound cleaning.

Patient What do I need to do now?

Doctor I will call Dr. Trujillo and **6**_____. She will visit your room shortly after you get checked in.

Patient OK, then I need to call my family and discuss this with them.

Doctor She is one of the best infectious disease specialists in town and will **7**_____ you.

Patient That's very comforting to hear. Thank you.

VOCABULARY

1 Please review the terms below. Draw lines to match each word to the correct definition.

1 What types of symptoms would a patient with Meniere's disease present with?

vertigo • a. ringing, buzzing, hissing, chirping, whistling, or other sounds in the ears

tinnitus • b. a feeling of dizziness and being unable to balance oneself

aural fullness • c. feeling like one's ear is blocked

2 What types of symptoms would a patient with meningitis present with?

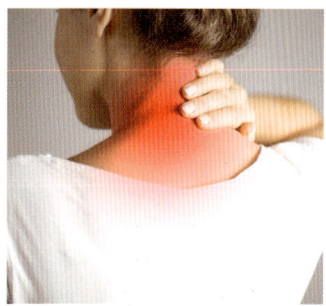

irritability • a. patches of skin that are discolored

stiff neck • b. soreness and difficulty moving the neck, especially when trying to turn the head to the side

blotchy skin • c. a feeling of agitation

3 What types of symptoms would a patient with cellulitis have?

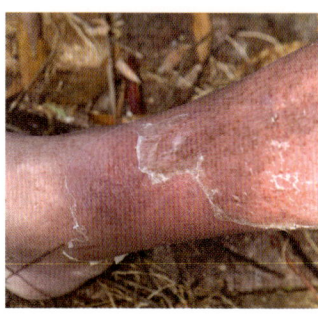

swelling • a. raised, curved shape on the surface of the body which appears as a result of an injury or an illness

warmth • b. a small pocket of body fluid (lymph, serum, plasma, blood, or pus) within the upper layers of the skin

blister • c. a feeling of an elevated temperature in the affected area

2 Read the sentences below and complete them with words from **1**.

1 Mr. Rosado, the ringing sound you are hearing is called _____. It's often very difficult to find the exact cause.

2 I have a very _____. I can't move my head at all.

3 Yes, I feel the _____ on my wound. It feels a little bit hot. I think it's infected.

3 Match the structures with the definitions (A-F).

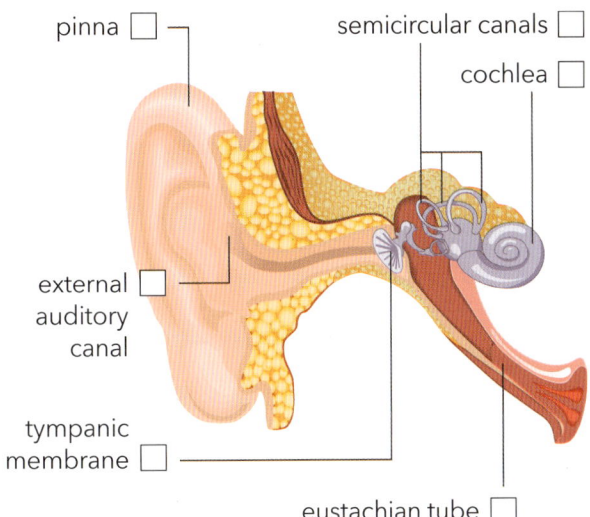

pinna ☐
semicircular canals ☐
cochlea ☐
external auditory canal ☐
tympanic membrane ☐
eustachian tube ☐

A. a twisted tube inside the inner ear that is the main hearing organ
B. a group of three fluid-filled tubes in the inner ear that are capable of detecting the rotational acceleration of the head
C. external part of the ear
D. also called an eardrum; a thin membrane that separates the middle ear from the external ear and vibrates when struck by sound waves
E. a tube that connects the middle ear with the upper part of the pharynx, serving to equalize air pressure on either side of the eardrum
F. auditory canal leading from the opening of the external ear to the eardrum

REVIEW

Review the patient's complaint and complete the medical chart.

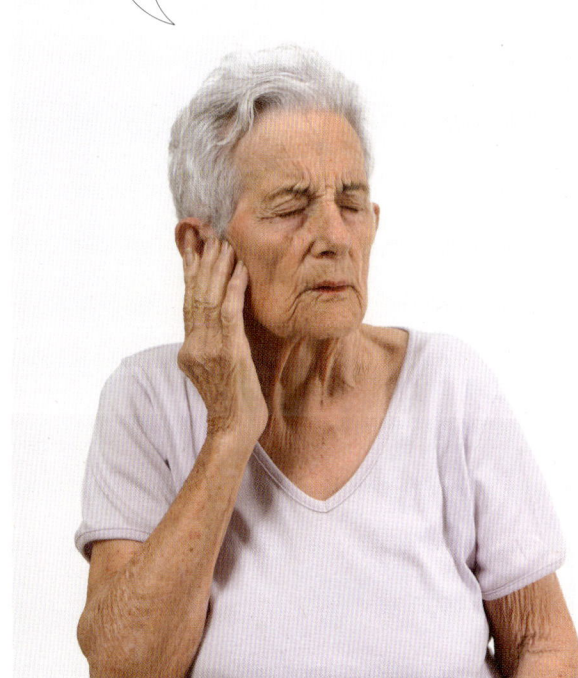

"I have a ringing sound in my ear and feel like I am spinning around. I have never felt like this before. I have always been healthy. All my family members are healthy as well."

**Patient Name:
Mia TAYLOR, 66-yr-old, F**

Chief complaint:
_____

Past medical history:
_____

Family history:
_____
_____

Social history: No current alcohol/drug use, occupation: retired

Review of systems: All other systems reviewed and normal

Unit 12 Discussing Referrals and Admission

LISTENING

1 🎧 Listen to the conversation between a doctor and a patient.

2 Read the following statements and mark the following as true (T) or false (F).

1. Mr. Orozco will have emergency surgery. _____
2. Mr. Orozco will need multidisciplinary team care. _____
3. An intensive care specialist will be the leader of the team. _____
4. An infectious disease specialist may start treatment with an antibiotic first. _____
5. Mr. Orozco has been ill for several months. _____

3 🎧 Listen again and choose the correct answers.

1. Which specialist does the doctor **NOT** mention during the conversation?
    a. pulmonologist
    b. nephrologist
    c. neurologist
    d. cardiologist

2. What is Mr. Orozco's working diagnosis?
    a. Meniere's disease
    b. sepsis
    c. acute appendicitis
    d. hypertension

3. Which medical condition does the doctor **NOT** mention during the conversation?
    a. hypotension
    b. pneumonia
    c. altered cognition
    d. diminished urine output

LANGUAGE POINT

1 Check how to use the expressions below and read the example sentences.

In my opinion, + Sentence.
: used to tell a patient what your opinion is
e.g. *In my opinion, it would be beneficial to consult an ENT specialist to check for eardrum damage.*
e.g. *In my opinion, you should see a pulmonologist to rule out the possibility of a lung infection.*

Note "I believe …" can also be used to tell a patient what you think or believe
e.g. *I believe you can monitor your own symptoms at home. You don't need any treatment at this stage.*
e.g. *I believe you will need to be admitted to lower your fever and start antibiotic treatment.*

2 Make a complete sentence by putting the words from the brackets in the correct order.

1. In my opinion, _____.
(the severity of your infection / we can only determine / after we receive your blood test results)

2. I believe _____.
(in the appendix, pancreas, and abdominal area / to view possible infections / you will need a CT scan)

3. In my opinion, _____.
(as your kidneys / dialysis might be required / are affected)

SPEAKING PRACTICE

1 With a partner, act out the roles below by using the expressions from Language Point. Then, switch roles.

Student A
You are the doctor. Discuss the topics below with Student B:
- reasons and benefits why a patient would need to see another specialist
- reasons why a patient needs to be admitted

Student B
You are the patient. Talk to Student A about your concerns regarding a referral or admission.

2 Below are some commonly mispronounced words. Listen carefully and repeat them out loud.

1. meningitis [men-in-**jahy**-tis]
2. Meniere's [meyn-**yairz**]
3. tinnitus [ti-**nuh**-tuhs]
4. peritonitis [per-i-tn-**ahy**-tis]

Unit 12 Discussing Referrals and Admission

Appendix

Parts of the Body ──────── 82

Commonly Used Medical Terms ──────── 88

Answer Key ──────── 90

Listening Scripts ──────── 103

Parts of the Body

UNIT 1

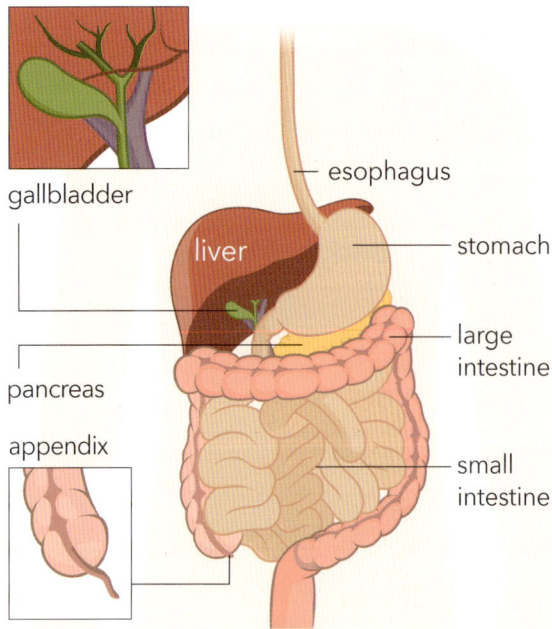

- **esophagus:** the muscular tube that carries food and liquids from the mouth to the stomach
- **pancreas:** the organ that plays an essential role in converting the food we eat into fuel for the body's cells
- **liver:** the organ that makes bile which helps carry away waste and breaks down fats in the small intestine during digestion
- **stomach:** the organ that starts the digestive process when food arrives here
- **gallbladder:** the organ that holds the digestive fluid called bile
- **large intestine:** also called the colon; part of the final stages of digestion
- **small intestine:** the organ that helps to further digest food coming from the stomach and absorbs most of the nutrients from what we eat and drink
- **appendix:** the organ which is located in the right lower abdomen; the removal of this organ causes no observable health problems

UNIT 2

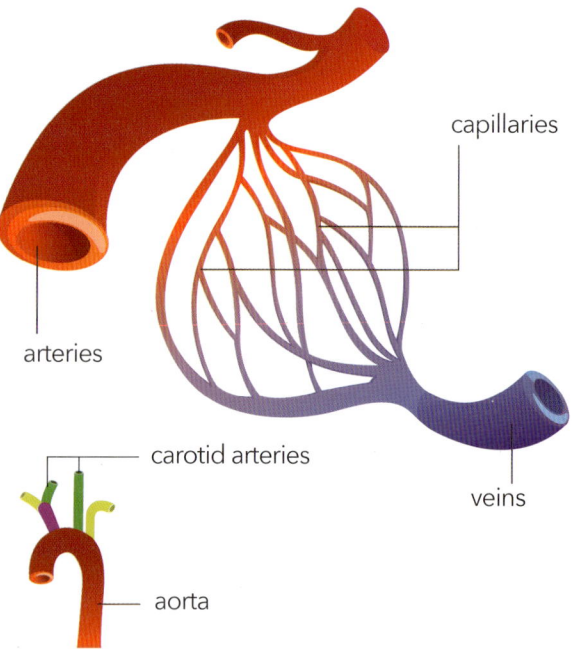

- **arteries:** blood vessels that deliver oxygen-rich blood from the heart to tissues in the body
- **capillaries:** small blood vessels that connect arteries to veins
- **veins:** vessels that carry blood towards the heart
- **aorta:** the largest artery in the heart
- **carotid arteries:** major blood vessels in the neck that supply blood to the brain, neck, and face

UNIT 3

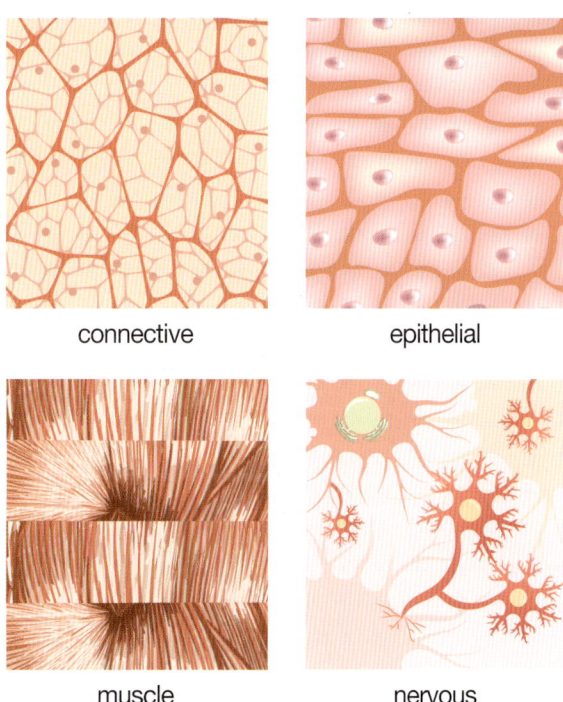

connective | epithelial
muscle | nervous

- **connective tissue:** tissues that provide support, bind together, and protect other tissues and organs in the body
- **epithelial tissue:** thin tissues that cover the exposed surfaces of the body
- **muscle tissue:** the only tissue in the body that has the ability to contract and therefore move the other parts of the body
- **nervous tissue:** tissue that monitors and regulates the functions of the body; found in the brain, spinal cord, and nerves

UNIT 4

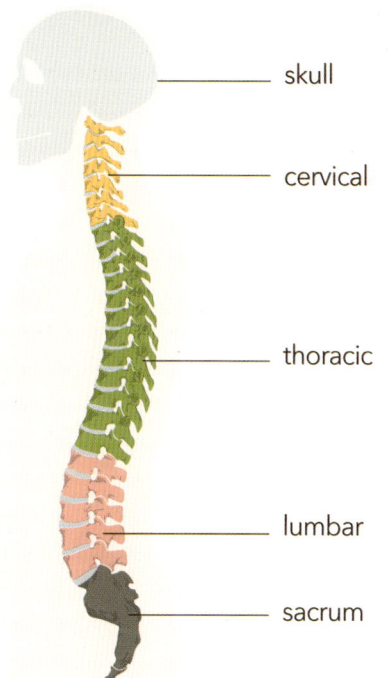

- **skull:** a framework of bone or cartilage that provides structure to the head and face while also protecting the brain
- **cervical:** bones that bear the weight of the body
- **thoracic:** bones that hold the rib cage and protect the heart and lungs
- **lumbar:** bones that support and promote the movement of the head and neck
- **sacrum:** bones that connect the spine to the hip bones

UNIT 5

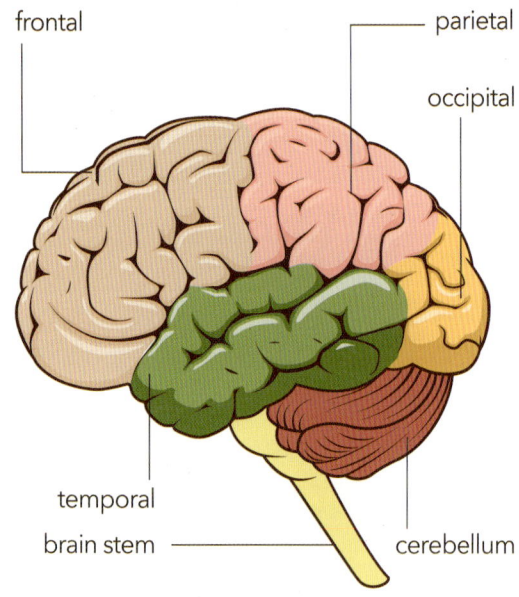

- **brain stem:** stem that coordinates motor control signals sent from the brain to the body, and regulates vital cardiac and respiratory systems
- **occipital:** lobe that is responsible for processing visual information from the eyes
- **parietal:** part of the brain that helps process the senses of touch and pain
- **cerebellum:** structure that plays a vital role in virtually all physical movement
- **frontal:** lobe that controls important cognitive skills in humans such as emotional expression, problem solving, memory, language, judgment, and sexual behaviors
- **temporal:** lobe that is involved with memory and hearing; processes information from our senses of smell, taste, and sound; plays a role in memory storage

UNIT 6

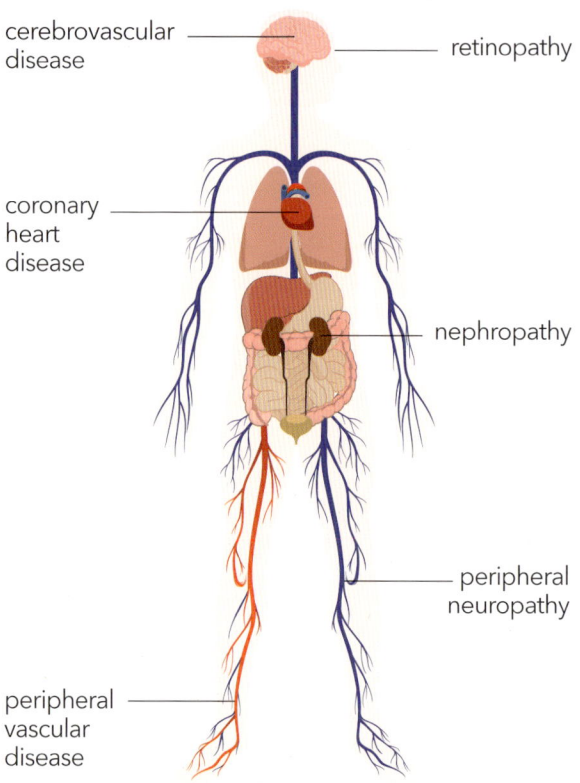

- **cerebrovascular disease:** a condition that temporarily or permanently limits or blocks blood flow to the brain
- **retinopathy:** any damage to the retinas that can cause vision loss and blindness
- **coronary heart disease:** narrowing or blockage of the coronary arteries causing a reduction of blood flow to the heart muscle
- **nephropathy:** a disease of the kidneys caused by damage to the small blood vessels or to the units in the kidneys that clean the blood
- **peripheral vascular disease:** a disease that causes restricted blood flow to the arms, legs, or other body parts and might cause potential loss of limbs
- **peripheral neuropathy:** damage or dysfunction of one or more nerves that typically results in numbness, tingling, muscle weakness, and/or pain in the affected area

UNIT 7

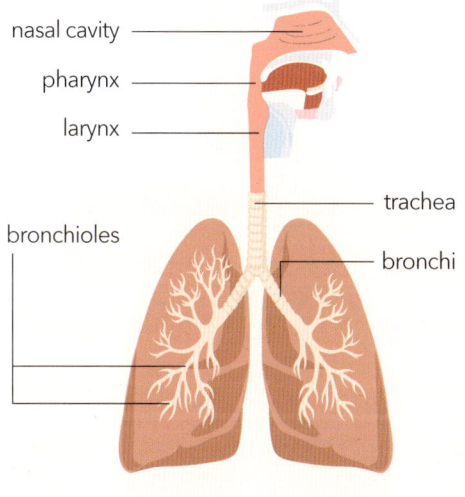

- **nasal cavity:** a large, air-filled space above and behind the nose, located in the middle of the face
- **pharynx:** the membrane-lined cavity behind the nose and mouth, connecting them to the esophagus
- **larynx:** a tube-shaped organ in the neck that contains the vocal cords
- **trachea:** a tube-like section of the respiratory tract that connects the larynx with the bronchial parts of the lungs
- **bronchi:** the large air passages that lead from the trachea (windpipe) to the lungs
- **bronchioles:** the tiny branches of air tubes within the lungs that are a continuation of the bronchus

UNIT 8

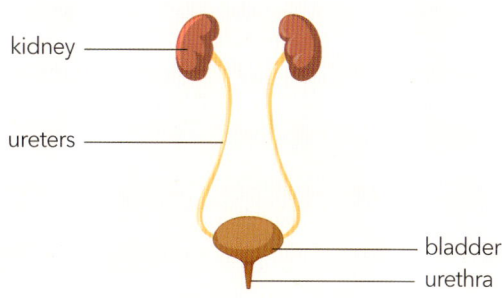

- **kidney:** two bean-shaped organs in the renal system which help the body pass waste as urine; filters blood before sending it back to the heart
- **ureters:** tubes that carry urine from the kidney to the bladder
- **bladder:** a round, bag-like organ that stores urine and is located in the pelvic area which is just below the kidneys and right behind the pelvic bone
- **urethra:** a tube that carries urine from the bladder to outside of the body

UNIT 9

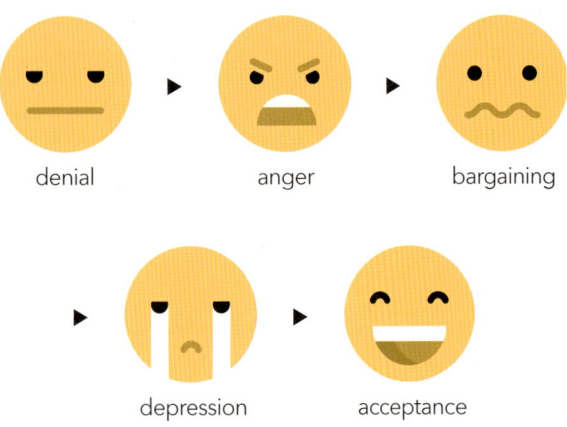

- **denial:** the stage in which the patient and their family do not believe the announcement of impending death and often believe that a mistake has been made in the diagnosis
- **anger:** the stage in which most people can't continue denying impending death or the loss of a loved one and denial soon gives way to feelings of anger, rage, jealousy, and hatred
- **bargaining:** the stage in which the patient tries to delay the end by bargaining in an attempt to avoid the unavoidable
- **depression:** the stage that focuses on a deep sense of loss and is felt in varying degrees from person to person
- **acceptance:** the final stage that is about accepting the new reality

UNIT 10

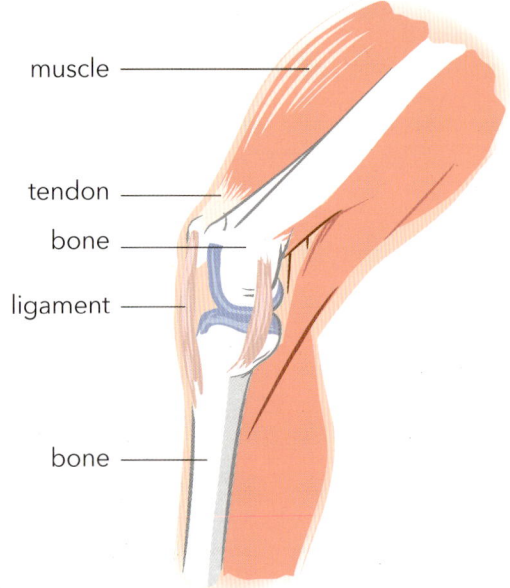

- **muscle:** a tissue composed of cells or fibers, the contraction of which produces movement in the body
- **tendon:** a fibrous connective tissue which attaches muscle to bones and serves to move the bones
- **bone:** structure that provides a rigid framework as well as support for other parts of the body; it plays an important role in the movement of the body and protects many of the internal organs
- **ligament:** a fibrous connective tissue that connects bones to other bones and gives the joints support while also limiting their movement

UNIT 11

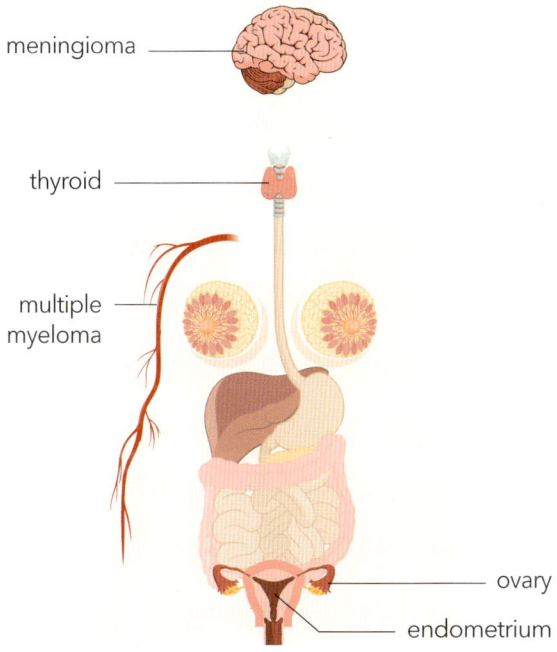

- **meningioma:** brain tumors that develop from the membrane (the "meninges") that covers the brain and spinal cord
- **thyroid:** a butterfly-shaped gland that is located at the front of the neck, below the Adam's apple, and makes a hormone that controls how fast the heart beats and how fast calories are burned
- **multiple myeloma:** a cancer that forms in a type of white blood cell called a plasma cell
- **endometrium:** the layer in which the implantation (the stage of pregnancy) takes place
- **ovary:** the organ that produces and releases eggs (oocytes) into the female reproductive tract at the mid-point of each menstrual cycle

UNIT 12

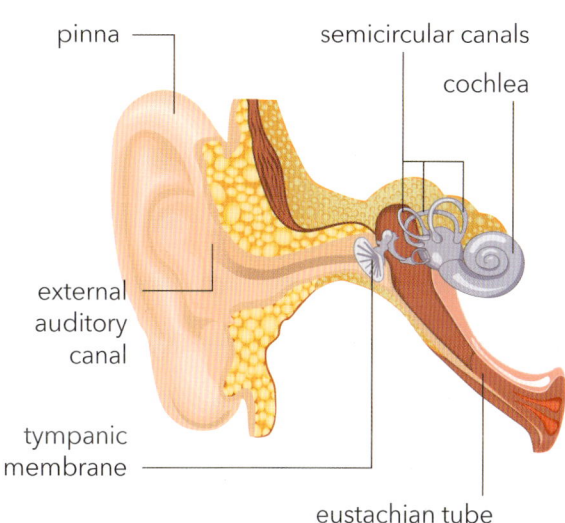

- **pinna:** external part of the ear
- **external auditory canal:** auditory canal leading from the opening of the external ear to the eardrum
- **tympanic membrane:** also called an eardrum; a thin membrane that separates the middle ear from the external ear and vibrates when struck by sound waves
- **semicircular canals:** a group of three fluid-filled tubes in the inner ear that are capable of detecting the rotational acceleration of the head
- **cochlea:** a twisted tube inside the inner ear that is the main hearing organ
- **eustachian tube:** a tube that connects the middle ear with the upper part of the pharynx, serving to equalize air pressure on either side of the eardrum

Commonly Used Medical Terms

A

ACUTE new, sudden, urgent pain or illness
ANTIBIOTIC drug that can kill bacteria and other microorganisms
ADVERSE EFFECT side effect, undesired reaction
ANAPHYLAXIS serious, possibly life-threatening allergic reaction
ANEMIA decreased healthy red blood cells
ANOREXIA eating disorder in which person will not eat; loss of appetite
ANTICONVULSANT drug for preventing seizures
ARRHYTHMIA abnormal heartbeat or any change from the regular heartbeat
ASPIRATION fluid entering the lungs, often after vomiting
ASTHMA lung disease in which the airways narrow and swell, making breathing difficult
ASYMPTOMATIC without symptoms

B

BENIGN not cancerous
BRADYCARDIA slow heartbeat
BRONCHOSPASM breathing trouble due to narrowing of the airways

C

CARCINOGEN any substance that causes cancer
CHEMOTHERAPY a drug treatment, most often used to treat cancer
CHRONIC continuing for a long time, long-lasting
COMA unconscious state in which a person cannot be awakened
CONGENITAL present before birth
CORONARY ATERY DEASE plaque in the heart's arteries that could lead to a heart attack
CULTURE test for organisms that could cause infection

D

DIURETIC drug that increases urination
DYSFUNCTION state of abnormal function
DYSPLASIA abnormal cells

E

EDEMA swelling, body parts swell from injury or inflammation
EMESIS vomiting
EPIDURAL outside the spinal cord
EXTERNAL outside the body

F

FIBRILLATION irregular heartbeat that can cause blood clots

G

GENERAL ANESTHESIA pain prevention by giving medications to cause a sleep-like state before a surgery or other medical procedure
GESTATION pregnancy, the time between conception and birth

H

HEMATOMA a bruise, a black or blue mark
HYPERTENSION high blood pressure
HYPOTENSION low blood pressure

I

INTRAMUSCULAR into the muscle; within the muscle
INTRAVENOUS (IV) through the vein
INTUBATE the process of inserting a tube into the airway

INVASIVE PROCEDURE puncturing, opening, or cutting the skin to gain access to the body

L
LAPAROTOMY surgical procedure in which an incision is made into the abdominal cavity to enable a doctor to examine the abdominal organs
LESION wound, damage, or injury in the tissue
LOCAL ANESTHESIA creation of insensitivity to pain in a specific part of the body, usually by injection of numbing medications

M
MALAISE a vague feeling of overall weakness; a feeling of discomfort
MALIGNANCY cancer or other progressively growing and spreading tumor, usually fatal if untreated
METASTASIS spread of cancerous tumor from one part of the body to another
MYALGIA muscle pain or ache
MYOCARDIAL INFARCTION heart attack

N
NONINVASIVE not cutting or entering the skin; not involving any invasive procedure

O
OCCLUSION closing or blockage of a blood vessel

P
PRENATAL before birth
PROPHYLAXIS treatment/drug given to prevent disease
PROGNOSIS probable outcomes or an opinion based on medical experience
PROSTHESIS artificial device that replaces a missing body part, most often limbs, such as arms or legs
RENAL pertaining to the kidneys

R
REGIMEN the course of a treatment
RELAPSE the return of a disease or a bad condition

S
SEDATIVE a drug to calm or make more relaxed
STUPOR almost unconscious state in which it is difficult to get a response to normal conversation
SUBCUTANEOUS under the skin
SUPINE lying on the back with the face upward

T
THROMBUS blood clot
TRAUMA injury; wound
TREADMILL running machine used to test heart function

V
VARICES abnormally enlarged veins
VASOSPASM narrowing of the blood vessels

Answer Key

UNIT 1

WARM UP 2

C → Course
O → Onset
D → Duration
I → Intensity
E → Exacerbating factors
R → Remitting factors
S → Symptoms

WARM UP 3

Chief complaint → e
Course → d
Onset → c
Duration → b
Intensity → h
Exacerbating → g
Remitting → a
Symptoms → f

EXPRESSIONS 1

1 → a
2 → g
3 → b
4 → h
5 → d
6 → c
7 → f
8 → e

EXPRESSIONS 2

1 brings … in
2 How long have … been going on
3 describe the pain
4 On a scale of 1 to 10
5 make them worse
6 Have you tried
7 spread to

VOCABULARY 1

1 sharp → b
  burning → a
  nagging → c
2 pressure-like → a
  stabbing → c
  tender to touch → b
3 throbbing → c
  squeezing → b
  dull → a

VOCABULARY 2

1 nagging
2 pressure-like
3 throbbing

VOCABULARY 3

Esophagus → A
Pancreas → B
Liver → C
Stomach → D
Gallbladder → E
Large intestine → F
Small intestine → G
Appendix → H

REVIEW

Chief complaint: stabbing pain on R abdominal
History of present illness: pain for 1 week
Past medical history: no history of signs and symptoms before

LISTENING 2

1 T
2 T
3 T
4 F
5 T

LISTENING 3

1 b
2 c
3 d

LANGUAGE POINT 2

1 tried
2 had
3 taking

UNIT 2

WARM UP 2

S → Signs / Symptoms
A → Allergies
M → Medications
P → Past pertinent medical history
L → Last menstrual cycle
E → Event leading up to present illness / injury

WARM UP 3

Signs / Symptoms → a
Allergies → b
Medications → c
Past pertinent medical history → d
Last menstrual cycle → e
Events leading up to present illness / injury → f

EXPRESSIONS 1

1 → a
2 → g
3 → d
4 → e
5 → h
6 → b
7 → i
8 → c
9 → f

EXPRESSIONS 2

1 I should know about
2 currently taking
3 work well to control
4 Have you had
5 the outcome
6 Do you have

VOCABULARY 1

1 conjunctivitis → b
  allergic rhinitis → c
  hives → a
2 confusion → c
  fatigue → a
  palpitations → b
3 heartburn → c
  indigestion → b
  nausea → a

VOCABULARY 2

1 hives
2 palpitations
3 nausea

VOCABULARY 3

Arteries → A
Capillaries → B
Veins → C
Aorta → D
Carotid arteries → E

REVIEW

Chief complaint: palpitations

Past medical history: no medications
Family history: Father has HTN

LISTENING 2

1 T
2 T
3 F
4 F
5 F

LISTENING 3

1 a
2 c
3 b

LANGUAGE POINT 2

1 allergies
2 food allergies
3 medications

UNIT 3

WARM UP 2

B ⇒ Blood pressure (high)
A ⇒ Arthritis / Alcoholism
L ⇒ Lung disease
D ⇒ Diabetes
C ⇒ Cancer
H ⇒ Heart disease
A ⇒ Arthritis / Alcoholism
S ⇒ Stroke
M ⇒ Mental health disorders

WARM UP 3

Blood pressure (high) ⇒ b
Arthritis ⇒ b
Lung disease ⇒ a
Diabetes ⇒ a
Cancer ⇒ a
Heart disease ⇒ a
Alcoholism ⇒ c
Stroke ⇒ b
Mental health disorders ⇒ c

EXPRESSIONS 1

1 ⇒ a
2 ⇒ e
3 ⇒ f
4 ⇒ c
5 ⇒ d
6 ⇒ b
7 ⇒ g

EXPRESSIONS 2

1 Would you please
2 any health issues like
3 Have you checked
4 Do you use
5 if you don't mind
6 What's … like

VOCABULARY 1

1 nipple retraction ⇒ b
  lump ⇒ a
  discharge ⇒ c
2 loss of appetite ⇒ c
  night sweats ⇒ b
  chills ⇒ a
3 blurred vision ⇒ a
  peripheral vision loss ⇒ c
  double vision ⇒ b

VOCABULARY 2

1 discharge
2 night sweats
3 blurred vision

VOCABULARY 3

Connective ⇒ A

Epithelial ➡ B
Muscle ➡ C
Nervous ➡ D

REVIEW

Family history: no FH
Social history: pt lives alone at home;
no alcohol, not stressed

LISTENING 2

1. F
2. T
3. F
4. T
5. F

LISTENING 3

1. b
2. d
3. d

LANGUAGE POINT 2

1. How
2. diet
3. work

UNIT 4

WARM UP 2

R ➡ Respiratory
U ➡ Urinary
N ➡ Nervous
M ➡ Muscular
R ➡ Reproductive
S ➡ Skeletal
L ➡ Lymphatic
I ➡ Integumentary
D ➡ Digestive
E ➡ Endocrine

C ➡ Cardiovascular

WARM UP 3

Respiratory ➡ c
Urinary ➡ b
Nervous ➡ a
Muscular ➡ d
Reproductive ➡ e
Skeletal ➡ h
Lymphatic ➡ g
Integumentary ➡ f
Digestive ➡ k
Endocrine ➡ j
Cardiovascular ➡ i

EXPRESSIONS 1

1 ➡ a
2 ➡ e
3 ➡ g
4 ➡ d
5 ➡ b
6 ➡ f
7 ➡ c

EXPRESSIONS 2

1. check … thoroughly
2. do you feel any
3. empty your bladder
4. Have you noticed
5. anything abnormal
6. any difficulty breathing
7. been diagnosed with

VOCABULARY 1

1. burning sensation ➡ c
   aching sensation ➡ b
   tingling sensation ➡ a
2. shooting pain ➡ b
   muscle ache ➡ a
   weakness ➡ c
3. acute ➡ a

Answer Key 93

intermittent ➡ c
chronic ➡ b

VOCABULARY 2

1 burning
2 shooting
3 chronic

VOCABULARY 3

Skull ➡ A
Cervical ➡ D
Thoracic ➡ C
Lumbar ➡ B
Sacrum ➡ E

REVIEW

Chief complaint: burning pain on back
Review of systems: no other signs and symptoms

LISTENING 2

1 T
2 F
3 T
4 F
5 T

LISTENING 3

1 d
2 d
3 c

LANGUAGE POINT 2

1 stuffed
2 bloating
3 tingly

UNIT 5

WARM UP 2

I ➡ Inspection
P ➡ Palpation
P ➡ Percussion
A ➡ Auscultation

WARM UP 3

Inspection ➡ a
Palpation ➡ c
Percussion ➡ b
Auscultation ➡ d

EXPRESSIONS 1

1 ➡ a
2 ➡ g
3 ➡ c
4 ➡ f
5 ➡ e
6 ➡ d
7 ➡ b

EXPRESSIONS 2

1 it seems
2 Let me
3 take a deep ..... in and out
4 Let's check
5 It should be
6 shortness of breath
7 may need to

VOCABULARY 1

1 tingling ➡ b
  numbness ➡ a
  tremor ➡ c
2 confusion ➡ a
  disoriented ➡ c
  slurred speech ➡ b
3 dehydration ➡ c
  shivering ➡ b

skin flushing ➡ a

VOCABULARY 2

1 numbness
2 disoriented
3 shivering

VOCABULARY 3

Brain stem ➡ A
Occipital ➡ B
Parietal ➡ C
Cerebellum ➡ D
Frontal ➡ E
Temporal ➡ F

REVIEW

Chief complaint: slurred speech
Review of systems: weakness on
R arm and leg

LISTENING 2

1 T
2 F
3 T
4 T
5 T

LISTENING 3

1 b
2 d
3 b

LANGUAGE POINT 2

1 extend
2 squeeze
3 roll up

UNIT 6

WARM UP 2

S ➡ Subjective
O ➡ Objective
A ➡ Assessment
P ➡ Plan

WARM UP 3

Subjective ➡ a
Objective ➡ d
Assessment ➡ c
Plan ➡ b

EXPRESSIONS 1

1 ➡ a
2 ➡ d
3 ➡ f
4 ➡ b
5 ➡ e
6 ➡ c

EXPRESSIONS 2

1 would like to
2 quite normal
3 you're going to
4 send you for
5 make sure
6 observe your symptoms
7 prescribe you
8 If you experience

VOCABULARY 1

1 frequent urination ➡ b
  increased thirst ➡ a
  extreme hunger ➡ c
2 slow-healing sores ➡ c
  irritability ➡ b
  fatigue ➡ a
2 drowsiness ➡ a
  seeing stars ➡ c

confusion ➡ b

VOCABULARY 2

1 increased thirst
2 slow-healing sores
3 seeing stars

VOCABULARY 3

Retinopathy ➡ A
Peripheral vascular disease ➡ B
Nephropathy ➡ C
Coronary heart disease ➡ D
Peripheral neuropathy ➡ E
Cerebrovascular disease ➡ F

REVIEW

Chief complaint: fatigue and frequent urination
Past medical history: hypertension
Family history: father diagnosed with diabetes at age 43

LISTENING 2

1 F
2 T
3 T
4 F
5 F

LISTENING 3

1 c
2 b, d
3 d

LANGUAGE POINT 2

1 will
2 won't
3 goes

UNIT 7

WARM UP 2

V ➡ Vascular
I ➡ Infections
N ➡ Neoplastic
D ➡ Degenerative
I ➡ Intoxication
C ➡ Congenital
A ➡ Auto-immune
T ➡ Traumatic
E ➡ Endocrine (metabolic)

WARM UP 3

Vascular ➡ a
Infections ➡ f
Neoplastic ➡ c
Degenerative ➡ g
Intoxication ➡ e
Congenital ➡ b
Auto-immune ➡ d
Traumatic ➡ h
Endocrine (metabolic) ➡ i

EXPRESSIONS 1

1 ➡ d
2 ➡ b
3 ➡ c
4 ➡ a
5 ➡ e
6 ➡ f

EXPRESSIONS 2

1 concerned about
2 with further tests
3 order … tests
4 can show us
5 that may be causing
6 take too long
7 by a lot of different reasons
8 in a little bit

VOCABULARY 1

1. sweating → c
   shivering → b
   bloody mucus → a
2. chest tightness → b
   wheezing → a
   shortness of breath → c
3. dry cough → a
   difficulty breathing → c
   persistent hiccups → b

VOCABULARY 2

1. bloody mucus
2. wheezing sound
3. persistent hiccups

VOCABULARY 3

Larynx → A
Pharynx → B
Nasal cavity → C
Trachea → D
Bronchioles → E
Bronchi → F

REVIEW

Chief complaint: shortness of breath
Past medical history: no PMH
Family history: father had a heart attack

LISTENING 2

1. T
2. F
3. F
4. T
5. T

LISTENING 3

1. c
2. a
3. a, c

LANGUAGE POINT 2

1. if you need any urgent treatment after the lab results come back
2. if you need a follow-up appointment
3. how the medications help you

UNIT 8

WARM UP 2

A → Appendicitis
B → Biliary tract disease
D → Diverticulitis
O → Ovarian disease
M → Malignancy
I → Intestinal obstruction
N → Nephritic disorders
A → Acute pancreatitis
L → Liquor (ethanol)

WARM UP 3

Appendicitis → e
Biliary tract disease → g
Diverticulitis → b
Ovarian disease → d
Malignancy → i
Intestinal obstruction → a
Nephritic disorders → c
Acute pancreatitis → f
Liquor (ethanol) → h

EXPRESSIONS 1

1 → d
2 → a
3 → b
4 → c
5 → g
6 → h
7 → e
8 → f

EXPRESSIONS 2

1 arrived
2 I suspected
3 there is evidence of
4 basically
5 the results are negative
6 to take at home
7 the full course of

VOCABULARY 1

1 urge to urinate → c
  burning feeling → b
  cloudy urine → a
2 flank pain → b
  foul-smelling urine → a
  vomiting → c
3 fluid retention → a
  seizures → c
  urinating less frequently → b

VOCABULARY 2

1 urge to urinate
2 urinating less frequently
3 vomiting

VOCABULARY 3

Bladder → A
Ureters → B
Kidney → C
Urethra → D

REVIEW

Chief complaint: Flank pain
Past medical history: UTI, kidney stone

LISTENING 2

1 F
2 T
3 F
4 F

5 F

LISTENING 3

1 c
2 b
3 d

LANGUAGE POINT 2

1 need
2 will need
3 need

UNIT 9

WARM UP 2

A → Affect flat
W → Weight change (loss or gain)
E → Energy, loss of
S → Sad feelings / Suicidal thoughts
O → Others (guilt, loss of pleasure, hopeless)
M → Memory loss
E → Emotional blunting

WARM UP 3

Affect flat → c
Weight change (loss or gain) → f
Energy, loss of → a
Sad feelings / Suicidal thoughts → d
Others (guilt, loss of pleasure, hopeless) → b
Memory loss → g
Emotional blunting → e

EXPRESSIONS 1

1 → c
2 → e
3 → d
4 → b
5 → a
6 → f
7 → g

EXPRESSIONS 2

1 sorry to hear
2 but unfortunately
3 discuss anything with
4 Please do
5 as soon as possible
6 please feel free
7 Again, I'm so sorry for

VOCABULARY 1

1 bad mood → c
  hopeless → a
  suicidal thoughts → b
2 constipation → b
  difficulty falling / staying asleep → c
  changes in appetite → a
3 sudden calmness → a
  withdrawal → c
  self-harmful behavior → b

VOCABULARY 2

1 hopeless
2 difficulty staying asleep
3 self-harmful behavior

VOCABULARY 3

Denial → C
Anger → B
Bargaining → A
Depression → D
Acceptance → E

REVIEW

Chief complaint: suicidal thoughts
Social history: cigarettes use, excessive alcohol use

LISTENING 2

1 F
2 T
3 F
4 F
5 T

LISTENING 3

1 d
2 b
3 d

LANGUAGE POINT 2

1 Would you come to see me for a follow-up in two days?
2 I would suggest that we talk again if you have any more concerns.
3 Would you agree to see a psychiatrist for treatments?

UNIT 10

WARM UP 2

D → Deformities & Discolorations
C → Contusions
A → Abrasions & Avulsion
P → Penetrations & Punctures
B → Burns
T → Tenderness
L → Lacerations
S → Swelling & Symmetry

WARM UP 3

Deformities & Discolorations → e
Contusions → g
Abrasions & Avulsion → a
Penetrations & Punctures → f
Burns → b
Tenderness → c
Lacerations → h
Swelling & Symmetry → d

EXPRESSIONS 1

1 → f
2 → e
3 → d
4 → a
5 → c
6 → b

EXPRESSIONS 2

1 there are … available
2 I recommend
3 who can oversee
4 it will help … with
5 suggest … should
6 teach … about
7 perform daily activities
8 questions or concerns

VOCABULARY 1

1 lethargy → b
  paleness → c
  panic attacks → a
2 an inability to bear weight → a
  loss of function → c
  acute pain → b
3 flashback → b
  nightmare → a
  feeling of isolation → c

VOCABULARY 2

1 panic attack
2 acute pain
3 nightmare

VOCABULARY 3

Muscle → A
Bone → B
Tendon → C
Ligament → D

REVIEW

Chief complaint: headache following a road traffic accident
Past medical history: no PMH

LISTENING 2

1 F
2 T
3 T
4 F
5 T

LISTENING 3

1 b
2 d
3 c

LANGUAGE POINT 2

1 necessary
2 hard
3 necessary

UNIT 11

WARM UP 2

W → Weight control
A → Alcohol reduction
S → Smoking cessation
H → Health promotion
E → Exercise
D → Diet

WARM UP 3

Weight control → a
Alcohol reduction → d
Smoking cessation → b
Health promotion → c
Exercise → f
Diet → e

EXPRESSIONS 1

1. d
2. a
3. b
4. f
5. c
6. e

EXPRESSIONS 2

1. you can do
2. healthy eating habits
3. give … plenty of
4. good to limit
5. stay active
6. sedentary time
7. no more than
8. easy to adjust

VOCABULARY 1

1. joint pain → b
   backache → c
   skin problems → a
2. heartburn → c
   irregular periods → a
   varicose veins → b
3. snoring → a
   low self-esteem → c
   increased sweating → b

VOCABULARY 2

1. joint paints
2. varicose veins
3. low self-esteem

VOCABULARY 3

Multiple myeloma → A
Thyroid → B
Endometrium → C
Meningioma → D
Ovary → E

REVIEW

Chief complaint: irregular periods, heartburn, and joint pains
Family history: parents have HTN and diabetes
Social history: smoke cigarettes and drink alcohol daily

LISTENING 2

1. T
2. F
3. T
4. F
5. T

LISTENING 3

1. b
2. d
3. a

LANGUAGE POINT 2

1. should
2. should
3. must

UNIT 12

WARM UP 2

S → Shivering, fever, or very cold
E → Extreme pain or general discomfort ("worst ever")
P → Pale or discolored skin
S → Sleepy, difficult to rouse, confused
I → "I feel like I might die."
S → Short of breath

WARM UP 3

Meningitis → f
Skin or soft tissue infection → c

Pneumonia → a
Catheter-related infection → d
Peritonitis → g
Urinary tract infection → b
Infection of unknown source → e

EXPRESSIONS 1

1 → d
2 → b
3 → f
4 → a
5 → c
6 → g
7 → e

EXPRESSIONS 2

1 responding to
2 refer … to
3 receive … intravenously
4 spread through
5 under close observation
6 arrange an admission
7 take good care of

VOCABULARY 1

1 vertigo → b
  innitus → a
  aural fullness → c
2 irritability → c
  stiff neck → b
  blotchy skin → a
3 swelling → a
  warmth → c
  blisters → b

VOCABULARY 2

1 tinnitus
2 stiff neck
3 warmth

VOCABULARY 3

Cochlea → A
Semicircular canals → B
Pinna → C
Tympanic membrane → D
Eustachian tube → E
External auditory canal → F

REVIEW

Chief complaint: vertigo, tinnitus
Past medical history: no FMH
Family history: no FH

LISTENING 2

1 F
2 T
3 T
4 T
5 F

LISTENING 3

1 c
2 b
3 c

LANGUAGE POINT 2

1 we can only determine the severity of your infection after we receive your blood test results
2 you will need a CT scan to view possible infections in the appendix, pancreas, and abdominal area
3 dialysis might be required as your kidneys are affected

Listening Script

UNIT 1

Doctor Good morning, Mrs. Smith.
Patient Good morning, doc.
Doctor What brings you in today, Mrs. Smith?
Patient I have belly pain.
Doctor When did it first start?
Patient 1 week ago.
Doctor How often are you feeling the pain?
Patient It comes and goes.
Doctor Has it been getting better, worse, or has it stayed about the same?
Patient It's been getting worse.
Doctor I am sorry to hear that. Is this the first time you've ever had pain like this in your stomach?
Patient Yes. I've never felt anything like this before.
Doctor How would you describe the pain?
Patient It's dull and aching, but it can be sharp at times.
Doctor Is it tender to touch?
Patient Maybe, I am not sure.
Doctor Can you point to where it hurts?
Patient (points to epigastric region) It's usually in this area.
Doctor On a scale of 1 to 10 with 10 being the worst, how bad is it?
Patient It ranges between 5 and 7. Right now it's about 5.
Doctor Does anything make it worse?
Patient After eating, it hurts more.
Doctor I see. Does anything make it better? Have you tried any meds?
Patient I've tried Tums, but it didn't help.
Doctor Are there any other symptoms associated with your belly pain?
Patient No, I don't think so. I may have had a fever last night, but I am not sure if that is related.

UNIT 2

Doctor Mr. Mansfield, I would like to ask you more questions. Would that be OK?
Patient Of course, doctor.
Doctor Mr. Mansfield, would you please tell me about your past medical history or any chronic illnesses you have?
Patient I had a heart attack 7 years ago and two stents were successfully inserted.

Doctor What was the outcome after the stents were put in?
Patient I haven't had any chest pains since the procedure and of course I see my cardiologist regularly for follow-ups.
Doctor Have you had any other major or minor surgery other than that?
Patient No. It was my first time to be admitted to the hospital.
Doctor Are you on any prescribed medications or over-the-counter drugs?
Patient I take blood thinners as prescribed by my cardiologist.
Doctor How is your blood pressure?
Patient Sorry, I forgot to mention about my hypertension. I also take medication to lower my blood pressure. I don't remember the name though.
Doctor That's fine. We will take your blood pressure today as well.
Patient I took it this morning and it was about 120 over 80.
Doctor Well, that's good but we will check it again.
Patient OK. Sounds good.
Doctor Do you have any allergic reactions to medications that I should know about?
Patient I don't have any allergies but I suffer from claustrophobia so I cannot do a CT or MRI without sedation.
Doctor That's good to know. Do you have any other allergies to food, pets, or anything else?
Patient I don't eat nuts.
Doctor Why is that?
Patient Whenever I eat nuts, I get rashes.
Doctor For how long have you had this allergy?
Patient It started when I was young.
Doctor Thank you for the information. Is there anything else you want to share?
Patient That's all.

UNIT 3

Doctor Mr. Boggs, I would like to ask you about your family history. Do you mind?
Patient No, I don't mind. You can ask me anything.
Doctor Does anyone in your family have any medical issues I should know about?
Patient My grandfather had a stroke 10 years ago. He passed away due to complications a year after that.
Doctor Have your parents or siblings experienced that same medical condition?
Patient No. Only my grandfather has had a stroke.
Doctor Can you think of anyone else in your family who has had any other long-term health problems?
Patient I think my grandfather had high blood pressure as well.
Doctor Thank you for the information. Now I would like to know if you use any alcohol, tobacco, or other illegal substances.
Patient No, doctor. I don't use anything.
Doctor That's very good. So no drugs in your system right now, correct?
Patient No. Nothing.
Doctor Who do you currently live with?
Patient I live with my wife and our three kids.
Doctor How old are your kids?

Patient The oldest one is 9 years old. The other two kids are twins and they are 6.
Doctor Does your wife work?
Patient No. She is a stay-at-home mom.
Doctor What's your home life like?
Patient It is pretty good! I spend as much time as possible with my family and try to be a good father.
Doctor Do you think you have any stress at home?
Patient No, doctor. I'm happy at home.
Doctor That's good to hear. Is there anything else you would like to tell me about?
Patient No. I have told you pretty much everything.
Doctor Thank you for sharing all this information.
Patient No problem, doc.

UNIT 4

Doctor Thank you for all the information about your family and your social history.
Patient No problem, doctor.
Doctor Now, I will ask you more about your body. Would that be OK?
Patient Yes, sure.
Doctor Other than your back pain, do you have any tingling sensations or numbness?
Patient Yes, actually I can feel a tingling in my left hand.
Doctor Have you experienced any coughing, sputum, or shortness of breath?
Patient I think I am breathing normally.
Doctor Do you have any chest pain or discomfort right now?
Patient No, I'm totally fine.
Doctor Have you had any headaches, or dizziness?
Patient I guess I have been a little bit dizzy, but nothing too terrible.
Doctor Did you have any discomfort when you emptied your bladder last time?
Patient No. It was completely normal.
Doctor Do you have any vaginal bleeding and what's your menstrual cycle duration and frequency?
Patient No bleeding. My menstrual cycle is always normal.
Doctor Do you feel any swelling in your lymph nodes?
Patient I don't think so, doctor.
Doctor Have you had any recent skin problems such as wounds or rashes?
Patient I have an old surgical wound on my stomach. But that's it.
Doctor Any diarrhea or constipation?
Patient No.
Doctor When did you have your last bowel movement?
Patient This morning. And it was normal.
Doctor Thank you for answering my questions.
Patient Thank you, doctor.

UNIT 5

Nurse Good morning, Ms. Lopez. I'm Rachael. How are you feeling today?
Patient Good morning, Rachael. I'm not doing very well. Something is not right.
Nurse I'm sorry to hear that. I'm going to take your vitals now. First I'm going to take your blood pressure and pulse.
Patient OK, whenever you are ready.
Nurse It's 100 over 60. That's a little low.
Patient Well, that would be normal for me. My blood pressure always runs like that.
Nurse I see. So you don't have any problems due to the low blood pressure?
Patient No, it has never caused me any issues.
Nurse Now I'm going to take your temperature.
Patient Sure.
Nurse It's normal. 36.7°C. Please wait here. Dr. Smith will see you shortly.
Patient Thanks, Rachael.

Doctor Good morning, Ms. Lopez. I heard you came in today because of weakness in your left side?
Patient Yes, it just started this morning.
Doctor Can you raise both arms above your head?
Patient (trying to raise her arms) I cannot raise my left arm.
Doctor Please squeeze my fingers with your hands as hard as you can.
Patient (trying to squeeze the doctor's fingers) This is all I can do.
Doctor I see that your left hand is much weaker. Do you feel numbness in any part of your body?
Patient Yes, my left hand feels numb.
Doctor Are you having any trouble with your vision?
Patient Yes, it is a little bit blurred.
Doctor I see. Now, I will listen to your heart, Ms. Lopez.
(after checking her heart sounds) Ms. Lopez, we are going to run some tests to rule out the possibility of a stroke.
Patient OK, I was worried that it might be a stroke.

UNIT 6

Doctor Mr. Greene, you came to visit me due to the slow-healing wound on your foot today, right?
Patient Yes, doctor. Is there anything I should be worried about?
Doctor Actually, after reviewing your physical exam results, I am concerned about your elevated blood sugar level.
Patient What does that have to do with my wound?
Doctor Slow-healing wounds are a common sign of diabetes.
Patient Do I have diabetes?
Doctor Well, your recent weight loss, extreme thirst, and increased appetite are all signs of diabetes.
Patient Oh, I didn't know that.

Doctor Also, you have a family history of it.
Patient Yes, that's true.
Doctor I'm worried about your diet and lifestyle.
Patient So what should I do?
Doctor Today, I'm going to clean your wound and give you some medications to prevent secondary infection.
Patient OK, thanks doctor.
Doctor But you must come back for a follow-up appointment.
Patient Why do I need another appointment?
Doctor We will discuss the lab results. If the lab results show elevated blood sugar levels, then I will write a prescription to manage that.
Patient Should I be worried about this?
Doctor No need to worry yet. Once we have the lab results, we will go through the possible treatment options.
Patient I see.
Doctor Let's finish cleaning up your wound now.
Patient Thank you. Please go ahead.
Doctor Do you have any further questions or concerns?
Patient You explained things well, so I am OK for now.
Doctor Good. I will see you tomorrow with the test results Mr. Greene.
Patient Thank you doctor. See you tomorrow.

UNIT 7

Doctor You are experiencing shortness of breath, chest tightness, and sweating?
Patient Yes, and I don't know why.
Doctor After I review all the physical exams and your medical history, I'm going to need to run some tests.
Patient Is that absolutely necessary?
Doctor Yes, we need to find out the exact cause, and I'd like to see if the issue is in your lungs or heart.
Patient What kind of tests do I need, doctor?
Doctor First, I'm going to send you for a chest X-ray so we can look at your lungs.
Patient OK. What else?
Doctor Then I will order a basic blood test and an EKG to see if there are any problems in your heart.
Patient The blood test can show heart problems?
Doctor Yes, it is a test called cardiac markers. These tests can show if you have a myocardial infarction.
Patient Do I need to do this today?
Doctor Yes, Mr. Daniels. I recommend we do these tests as soon as possible.
Patient Why is that?
Doctor If the results show something abnormal, you may need urgent treatment.
Patient Oh, I didn't realize that!
Doctor If you are ready, a nurse will assist you with these tests.
Patient When do I need to come back for the results?
Doctor No need to leave. You can wait here as it won't take too long to get the results.
Patient Should I be worried about all of this?

Doctor It can be serious, but we will find out the results shortly.
Patient OK. I am glad we will know everything soon.
Doctor If all the results are normal, you can go home and monitor yourself.
Patient I really hope there's nothing wrong!
Doctor We will see soon, Mr. Daniels.
Patient OK, doctor. Thank you for explaining everything.

UNIT 8

Doctor Hi, Mr. White. How is your back pain?
Patient Well, it's better with pain meds but it is still there.
Doctor OK, I have your test results here.
Patient That's good. What do you see?
Doctor First of all it's not appendicitis, which is good.
Patient That is good to hear, doctor.
Doctor And I don't see any abnormalities in your intestinal organs.
Patient So what do you think is causing the pain?
Doctor When we first checked the X-ray, we didn't see the small kidney stones that are there.
Patient Kidney stones?
Doctor Yes, if you look at this CT image, can you see the small stones here? (showing the CT film)
Patient Oh, yes. I can see them.
Doctor This is what is causing your pain.
Patient I see. So my diagnosis is kidney stones?
Doctor Yes, that's correct and you will be fine once the stones are removed.
Patient Will I need surgery to remove them?
Doctor No. Your stones are relatively small, so they will pass naturally.
Patient Oh really? I don't need any treatment then?
Doctor You will need to drink at least 2 to 3 liters of water a day to help flush them out.
Patient OK. What about the pain? Will you give me any medication?
Doctor I will prescribe a pain reliever and also another medication that will help aid the passing of your stones.
Patient OK. That would be great.
Doctor Mr. White, please also reduce the amount of salt you consume.
Patient Why is that?
Doctor It will help prevent you from developing more kidney stones in the future.
Patient I see. Thank you for your advice, doctor.

UNIT 9

Doctor How are you feeling, Ms. Ann?
Patient I feel terrible.

Doctor Would you mind telling me more about what happened this morning?
Patient Well, doctor, it's quite a private matter.
Doctor I'm sure it is. But I'm here to help you and I don't want to assume anything.
Patient Erm… I'm just feeling so hopeless.
Doctor I'm so sorry to hear that. Please continue.
Patient I've started having suicidal thoughts.
Doctor Have you experienced any major life changes recently?
Patient I got divorced about a year ago and my mother passed away a few months ago.
Doctor It sounds like you have been going through a difficult time.
Patient I lost my appetite and also feel such a lack of energy these days.
Doctor Have you talked to anyone about your emotions or tried to get professional help?
Patient No. I'm alone and no one can help me.
Doctor I understand you are having a hard time. Let's see if we can help you find a way to cope with it all.
Patient I just don't know how I can avoid these suicidal thoughts.
Doctor I would recommend seeing a psychiatrist first. There are many types of medication that can help reduce your symptoms.
Patient Well, I don't know about taking medication. Are there any other options?
Doctor I would suggest psychological counseling then. You can explore the issues that cause you to feel suicidal and discover skills to help control your emotions more effectively.
Patient OK, doctor. That second choice sounds like the best one for me.
Doctor If you find yourself starting to feel again, would you please seek help right away?
Patient OK. I feel so silly about all of this. I will try to act sooner if I feel this way again.
Doctor I will give you a list of some psychologists in the area, as well as a referral letter.
Patient Thank you. Is there anyone you would personally recommend?
Doctor Dr. Linton is a colleague of mine. I could call him in advance if you wish.
Patient Oh, that would be so helpful. I really appreciate it.

UNIT 10

Doctor Ms. Woodmansee, I reviewed the X-ray and confirmed that your mother has a hip fracture.
Daughter Oh no! How bad is it?
Doctor Not too bad, but I would like to discuss some treatment options with you first.
Daughter Of course. I'm listening.
Doctor Your mother is 90 years old and currently has other diagnoses like dementia, pneumonia, and hypertension.
Daughter Yes, she is very weak and has a lot of health issues.
Doctor We need to consider hip surgery but it's a major surgery and there can be some complications.
Daughter Like what?
Doctor There is an increased risk of blood clots, confusion, infection, stroke, heart attack, and so on.
Daughter What happens if we don't fix the fracture with surgery?
Doctor If the bone doesn't heal, then she could experience swelling or tenderness, and the pain will likely worsen over time.

Daughter How long would she need to stay hospitalized after the surgery?
Doctor Because of her age and current conditions, it's hard to answer that. It will depend on how quickly your mother heals and regains mobility.
Daughter What will it take to achieve that?
Doctor She will do a few hours of physiotherapy every day until she is able to walk for longer distances.
Daughter I see. So, do you think surgery is the best treatment option?
Doctor It is a good option but with her current condition we may have to wait until she recovers from the pneumonia.
Daughter How long do we need to wait?
Doctor We are treating her with antibiotics, so we will need to observe the effects of the medication for a while.
Daughter OK. I will have to discuss all this with my mother and our family.
Doctor If it would help, I can meet with them as they may have other questions about the surgery plan and possible complications.
Daughter That would be great doctor. Can we meet tomorrow morning?
Doctor Yes, I will be here around 10am.
Daughter Thank you again.
Doctor Your mother should be fine and we will do our best to get her healed.
Daughter That's very comforting. I will see you tomorrow then.

UNIT 11

Doctor Mr. Higdon, your current symptoms of joint pain, increased sweating, backache, and heartburn are all related to your weight gain.
Patient Well, lately I haven't been very concerned about my health.
Doctor It is important that you recognize your condition and try to improve it before it gets more serious.
Patient Is it really that bad?
Doctor Yes, you are obese and have diabetes and all your symptoms stem from those issues.
Patient I'm so surprised to hear that all of my symptoms are related.
Doctor You will need to adjust your lifestyle before it becomes too complicated.
Patient What do you mean by that?
Doctor For example, if your diabetes remains uncontrolled, then you can develop vision problems, kidney disease, nerve damage, and much more.
Patient I didn't know that. I should do a better job of monitoring my blood sugar.
Doctor Also, obesity can put you at high risk for having other chronic illnesses such as joint problems, sleep apnea, heart disease, and so on.
Patient Oh, I guess I'm in trouble.
Doctor I strongly suggest you consider a lifestyle change.
Patient How can I change my lifestyle?
Doctor You can start with some diet modifications. For example, you can reduce your intake of sugar, fast food, and junk food and add grains, vegetables, fruits, beans, and dairy products to your diet instead.
Patient That will be challenging but I should try.
Doctor Also, you must stop smoking and consuming alcohol.
Patient I will consider it. Anything else?

Doctor You will need to increase the amount of your physical activity and avoid sedentary time as much as possible.
Patient What kinds of exercise do you recommend?
Doctor How about walking, jogging, swimming, or even water aerobics?
Patient I think jogging should be manageable.
Doctor Just remember that your main goals should be to lower your cholesterol level, drop the extra weight, and become more active.
Patient I got it, doctor. Thank you for your advice.

UNIT 12

Doctor Mrs. Orozco, I'm sorry to tell you this, but your husband's condition is very critical right now.
Wife What's happening to him?
Doctor Your husband has severe sepsis and needs to be admitted to an intensive care unit immediately.
Wife Oh, no. That sounds so serious!
Doctor Yes, it is. We found that the infection has already spread to other organs throughout his body.
Wife So, what kind of treatment does he need?
Doctor In my opinion, he will need multidisciplinary team care, which means several physicians will work together to deliver comprehensive care.
Wife How many doctors are we talking about?
Doctor I will first refer your husband to an intensive care specialist who will be the leader of our team.
Wife What happens after that?
Doctor The intensive care specialist will assess your husband and then decide treatment options.
Wife Can you explain this to me more? I'm so worried about my husband.
Doctor I believe that the intensive care specialist, the team leader, will be recommending that your husband sees an infectious disease specialist to get some antibiotic treatments started. We will have to wait and see what is recommended.
Wife What else do I need to know?
Doctor Your husband should also see a pulmonologist, nephrologist, and cardiologist.
Wife Would you tell me the reasons for each, please?
Doctor Your husband is experiencing shortness of breath and also pneumonia, so a pulmonologist will evaluate his lungs.
Wife I see. What about the others you mentioned?
Doctor Your husband's urine output is not at a normal level. A nephrologist will need to check for any kidney damage.
Wife OK, that sounds like a good plan so far, and what about the cardiologist?
Doctor His blood pressure is very low and a cardiologist can recommend further treatment options.
Wife I cannot believe how quickly his condition has worsened. He was so healthy just a week ago.
Doctor This is because the infection spread to other organs. Our experienced physicians will take good care of him.
Wife I really hope so.
Doctor I will make a few calls and make arrangements. Do you have any other questions or concerns?
Wife No, doctor. Thank you for all your explanations.